A MOVEABLE FEAST

Delicious food to take with you

KATY HOLDER

A
MOVEABLE
FEAST

Delicious food
to take with you

KATY HOLDER

hardie grant publishing

This book is dedicated
to my family near and far.
To those closest to me – Alex,
Max and Jack – and to my mum and
dad, and Emma and Simon, who are a
little further away but who inspired
in me, and still share with me,
a love of good food
and cooking.

CONTENTS

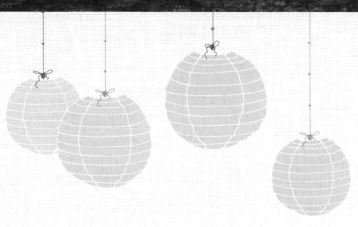

INTRODUCTION

THE IDEA FOR THIS BOOK came to me over the course of a few months as I planned outdoor adventures with my family, including days out with friends, short camping trips and picnics in the park; or we were asked to 'bring a plate' to a friend's house. As a stylist and recipe writer I always think about how the finished dish will look when I'm writing a recipe. But on these various excursions it occurred to me that for recipes cooked at home and then eaten elsewhere, extra thought needs to be given not only to how to transport the dish, but also to whether it will still taste good once it's cold. Food can do strange things when it cools down!

There are numerous occasions when you might need recipes that travel well. Maybe you've been asked to bring a plate to someone's house or you're planning a picnic at the races. Perhaps you're going on a hike and would like something tasty and filling for the end of your walk, or you simply want to eat outside in your garden because it's a beautiful summer's day. Whatever the occasion, *A Moveable Feast* is full of inspiring recipes that look and taste great, and travel well, with lots of tips on how best to transport your creations so they arrive at their destination in one piece.

Katy Holder

STYLING YOUR
MOVEABLE FEAST

THIS BOOK IS MORE than just a recipe book. It's also full of simple but effective ideas that show you how to personalise your table setting or picnic. Seek inspiration from the world around you or objects that you already have in your home. Be inspired by nature. This can be as simple as placing some beautiful weathered branches in the centre of your table, or using a smooth river pebble to prevent your paper napkins flying away in the wind.

I'm a huge fan of typography and have a set of alphabet stamps that I use in myriad ways – to stamp a name on a luggage tag to tie around a napkin, to write fun words on a smooth stone or to create sweet messages to attach to Christmas gifts. Another source of inspiration for me is second-hand markets when I'm travelling. I look for old books written in different languages and use the pages as placemats, drinks mats or as the base for a table decoration.

Do you collect anything? Once again look for inspiration in what you already have. A few pieces of vintage cutlery will add instant glamour or quirkiness to the table. Or why not make colourful napkin rings out of buttons tied together? I have a collection of teaspoons that I bring out for afternoon tea; I love the fact that none of them match and I have fond memories of where each one was bought.

Old glass bottles and mason jars can be used in a multitude of ways. Use them to transport food or to hold a flower arrangement, fill them with pretty or colourful sweets, or serve drinks in them. They don't even have to be old – some drinks come in gorgeous bottles that make cute vases. Lots of small bottles holding just one or two flower stems each can create a bigger impact than one large floral arrangement.

Baking paper, old-fashioned twine and coloured string add an old-world charm to picnics and table settings. Instead of simply wrapping sandwiches or rolls in foil, wrap them in baking paper and tie with beautiful string; when you hand them out it's like you're handing over a homemade gift to unwrap.

So now there's nothing stopping you. Organise a brunch or a picnic, or gather some friends for a beautiful afternoon tea, but most of all have fun and get together with friends and family – one of the most important things in life.

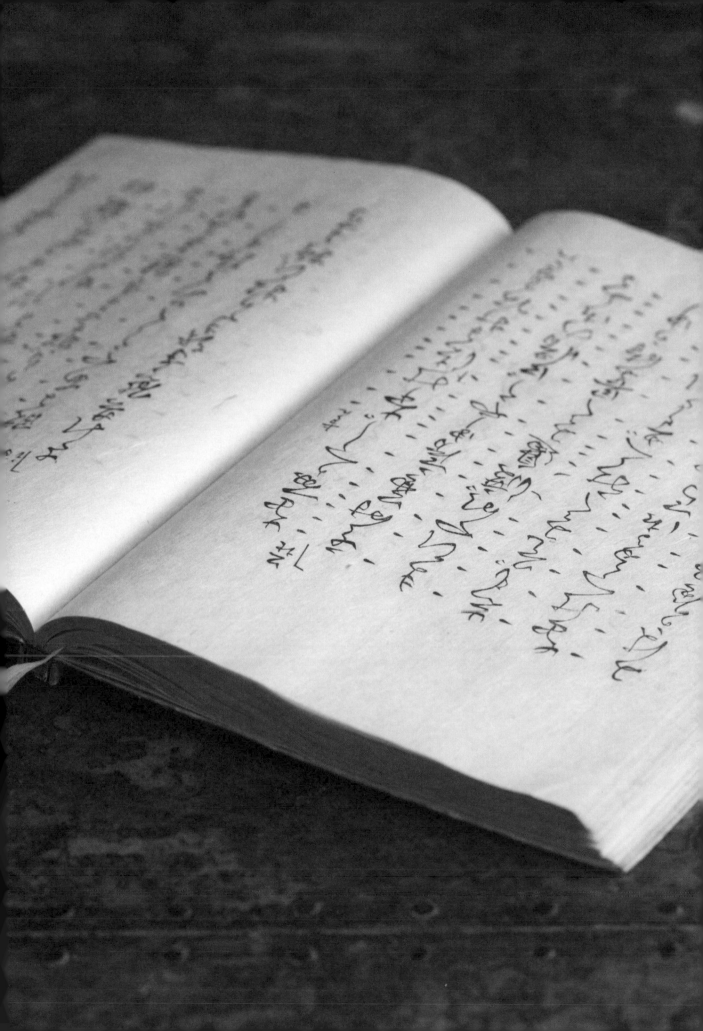

TRANSPORTING YOUR MOVEABLE FEAST

TRANSPORTING YOUR COOKED or pre-prepared dish is often the trickiest part of a picnic or bring-a-plate occasion. There's nothing worse than lovingly preparing a dish to find it's fallen apart or been damaged while you're on the move. Throughout this book I've made suggestions on how best to transport dishes to avoid such scenarios.

In general, if transporting pies, tartlets and cakes, cool them on a wire rack then return them to the tin for moving; this will help prevent damage while on the move, particularly to fragile pastry. Wrap sandwiches in layers of baking paper and tie the ends with coloured twine or string, then wrap them again in a layer of foil to prevent leakage. Remove just the layer of foil before serving.

It's often a better idea to cut cakes, pies and tortillas on arrival. However, if this isn't possible, transport individual pieces between layers of baking paper, padded with paper towel if necessary.

Ensure containers carrying liquids, such as sauces or salad dressings are leak-proof; wrap them in a layer of plastic wrap to be extra safe. On the subject of salads, don't dress them too far in advance, otherwise the leaves will become soggy. Transporting the salad components separately before tossing everything together at the last minute will ensure your salad looks its best when served.

Transport drinks in flasks or plastic bottles, then transfer them to beautiful jugs or individual cute bottles to serve.

Always remember to keep things cool in an esky (cool box) and out of the sun. Never leave food in the back of a hot car and when you arrive at your destination always look for the coolest or shadiest spot to put your food.

Think about how you're going to serve your food and see if this can make transportation easier. Why not divide a salad between individual cardboard noodle boxes (available from most craft shops) before you leave home, and then dress the salads just before serving? The boxes will help protect the salad leaves, but make sure you don't squash the leaves into the boxes. Serving food in jars is also a way to protect it. Salads, pâtés and drinks can all be served this way. Ensure the jars are leak-proof and protect them by wrapping them in cloth napkins or tea towels for the journey.

With a little forethought, you'll never arrive at your destination with anything but a beautiful dish.

Sophia

Loaves, BREADS and MUFFINS

HAVING A PICNIC with family and friends is a great way to get everyone together without one person having to do all the cooking and washing up. Just ask everyone to bring a plate of tasty nibbles – et voilà!

The loaves, breads and muffins in this chapter are ideal picnic fare, but they work equally well for brunch in the garden if you're not up for a picnic. The feta and herb bread rolls are super quick to make, and kids will love the corn and bacon polenta 'muffins'. For a sweet bite, the banana and roasted strawberry bread goes down a treat.

ZUCCHINI *and* RICOTTA LOAF

MAKES 6–8 SLICES

If you're looking for something a little different to take on a picnic – or even to pack in your lunchbox – give this recipe a go. It's not tricky to make and it transports well.

300 g (2 cups) self-raising flour
2 tablespoons flat-leaf parsley,
    finely chopped
2 teaspoons thyme leaves,
    finely chopped
1 teaspoon dried oregano
150 g ricotta
4 free-range eggs, lightly beaten
125 ml (½ cup) milk
70 g sun-dried tomatoes, drained
    and finely chopped
2 (250–300 g) zucchini
    (courgettes), grated
1 avocado, sliced, to serve

1 Line a loaf tin (approximately 22 x 8 cm) with baking paper. Preheat fan-forced oven to 170°C (190°C conventional/Gas 5).

2 Combine the flour, parsley, thyme and oregano in a large bowl.

3 Put the ricotta into a separate bowl and whisk in the eggs until well combined. Then whisk in the milk. Stir in the sun-dried tomatoes and zucchini and season well with sea salt and freshly ground black pepper.

4 Add the ricotta mixture to the flour mixture and stir to combine. Pour into the prepared tin and bake for 35 minutes. Then cover with foil and continue to cook for a further 25 minutes or until a skewer comes out clean when inserted. Leave to cool in the tin for 10 minutes then turn out onto a wire rack to cool completely.

5 Return to the tin to transport. Serve with avocado and freshly ground black pepper.

☞ **TIP** If you have any loaf leftover, pop a slice in the toaster or under the grill then spread with butter or avocado.

SALTED PARMESAN GRISSINI
with OLIVE TAPENADE

MAKES 32 GRISSINI

Yes, you can buy grissini from the shops, but let me tell you: these taste about a hundred times better!

7 g dry yeast or 1 x 7 g sachet
1 teaspoon sugar
550 g (3⅔ cups) plain
    (all-purpose) flour
1 teaspoon table salt
75 g parmesan cheese, finely grated
3 tablespoons olive oil, plus extra
    for greasing
1 tablespoon sea salt flakes

OLIVE TAPENADE
125 g pitted kalamata olives
1 tablespoon olive oil
1 garlic clove, crushed
1 tablespoon capers
2 anchovy fillets

1 Put 310 ml (1¼ cups) of warm water into a medium bowl. Sprinkle the yeast and sugar over the water and stir to dissolve. Set the mixture aside for 5 minutes, until it is frothy. (If it doesn't froth, the yeast is 'dead', so start again with a fresh packet.)

2 Sieve the flour and table salt into a large bowl and stir in the parmesan. Make a well in the centre of the mixture, then pour in the oil and the yeast mixture. Using your hands, gradually incorporate the flour into the liquid to eventually form a dough.

3 If you have a mixer with a dough hook, turn the mixer to low–medium speed and knead the dough for about 5 minutes, until smooth. Alternatively, put the dough onto a floured surface and knead for about 10 minutes, until smooth. Place the dough in a lightly oiled bowl, cover with a tea towel and leave in a warm place for about 1 hour, until the dough has risen and pretty much doubled in size.

4 Preheat fan-forced oven to 180°C (200°C conventional/ Gas 6). Lightly grease two or three large baking trays. Once the dough has risen, punch the centre then knead again for 1 minute. Divide dough into four equal portions then divide each portion into eight. Roll each smaller portion to about 20 cm in length. Arrange 1 cm apart on the trays. Brush with water, then sprinkle liberally with the sea salt flakes.

5 Bake for 15–20 minutes or until the grissini have risen and are golden. Serve warm or cold. Store in an airtight container until needed.

6 To make the tapenade, put all the ingredients in a small food processor and blend until smooth. Transfer to a lidded container and put in the fridge until needed. Note: depending on how long it sits in the fridge, the oil in the tapenade may solidify. As soon as it warms slightly it will liquefy again.

GOATS CHEESE, BLACK OLIVE and HERB MUFFINS

MAKES 12 MUFFINS

These are best eaten on the day they're made, however, if you do have any left over, warm them up and serve with some butter the next day.

2 free-range eggs, lightly beaten
220 ml milk
150 ml olive oil, plus extra
　for greasing
300 g (2 cups) self-raising flour
1 teaspoon sea or table salt
120 g pitted kalamata olives,
　finely chopped
3 tablespoons flat-leaf parsley,
　finely chopped
150 g goats cheese, crumbled
1 red chilli, deseeded and finely
　chopped (optional)

1　Preheat fan-forced oven to 180°C (200°C conventional/ Gas 6). Grease a 12-hole (capacity 80 ml or ⅓ cup) muffin tin or line with cupcake cases.

2　Combine the eggs, milk and olive oil in a bowl. Sift the flour and salt over the egg mixture then stir gently to combine. Fold in the olives, parsley, goats cheese and chilli and season with freshly ground black pepper.

3　Divide the mixture between the muffin holes and bake for 20–25 minutes until the muffins have risen and are golden.

4　Leave to cool for 5 minutes in the tin then transfer to wire racks to cool further.

☛ STYLING TIP

Balls of coloured and textured twine look beautiful stacked in glass jars and are handy for wrapping sandwiches and muffins for lunches.

BANANA and ROASTED STRAWBERRY BREAD with RICOTTA

MAKES 6–8 SLICES

Roasting strawberries intensifies their sweetness. I love this bread spread with a little ricotta, but it's delicious served without too.

250 g strawberries,
  hulled and halved
1 tablespoon balsamic vinegar
160 g caster sugar
3 ripe bananas, well mashed
2 free-range eggs, lightly beaten
200 g plain (all-purpose) flour
1 teaspoon table salt
1 teaspoon bicarbonate of soda
150 g ricotta (optional)

STYLING TIP

Keep the styling simple with a small flower and some pretty twine.

1 Preheat fan-forced oven to 180°C (200°C conventional/ Gas 6). Line a loaf tin (about 22 x 8 cm, or similar size) with baking paper.

2 Put the strawberries in a small roasting tin, drizzle with the vinegar and sprinkle with 2 tablespoons of the sugar. Roast for 15 minutes, until softened. Cool for 10 minutes.

3 Put the bananas in a large bowl and mix in the eggs. Sift in the flour, salt and bicarbonate of soda then stir in the remaining sugar. Gently fold through the strawberries and any cooking juices.

4 Transfer the mixture to the lined tin and bake for 50 minutes (if it starts to brown too quickly, cover with foil). Cover the top with foil then cook for a further 10 minutes. To ensure the loaf is cooked, stick a skewer into it and leave for 5 seconds then remove. If the skewer comes out dry, the bread is cooked.

5 Cool in the tin for 5 minutes, then turn out onto a wire rack to cool further. Serve warm or at room temperature, spread with a little ricotta.

UPSIDE-DOWN APPLE *and* ALMOND MUFFIN–CAKES

MAKES 12 MUFFIN–CAKES

I can't decide if these are muffins or cakes, but either way they are very yummy. They're quite rustic looking but this adds to their charm. Serve them for morning tea, for Mother's Day or on a lazy afternoon picnic.

1 small apple
vegetable oil for greasing
50 g butter
100 g golden syrup
2 teaspoons vanilla extract
80 g plain (all-purpose) flour
100 g ground almonds
1 teaspoon baking powder
½ teaspoon ground cardamom
   (optional)
3 free-range egg whites
120 g caster sugar
2 free-range egg yolks

1 Peel and core the apple then cut it into 5 mm thick slices. Cut each slice into bite-sized pieces. Line each hole of a 12-hole (capacity 80 ml or ⅓ cup) muffin tin with foil, smoothing the sides then lightly grease them.

2 Put the butter, golden syrup and 1 teaspoon of the vanilla extract into a small saucepan and cook over medium heat for about 2 minutes, until combined and starting to bubble. Divide the mixture between the muffin holes, then arrange the apple pieces on top.

3 Preheat fan-forced oven to 170°C (190°C conventional/ Gas 5). Combine the flour, ground almonds, baking powder and cardamom in a large bowl.

4 Put the egg whites into a separate bowl and, using an electric hand mixer, whisk until soft peaks form. Gradually add the sugar to the egg whites, whisking well after each addition to ensure the sugar dissolves. Then whisk in the egg yolks and the remaining 1 teaspoon of vanilla extract.

5 Using a large metal spoon, gently fold half the flour mixture into the egg mixture until just combined; do not overmix. Fold in the remaining flour mixture. Spoon the mixture into the prepared muffin tin, smoothing the tops.

6 Bake for 15–20 minutes or until golden brown and a skewer comes out clean after insertion. Cool in the tin for about 10 minutes, then carefully peel off the foil from each muffin, scraping any syrup left behind on the foil back onto the muffin. Turn upside down so the apples are on top, and leave to cool on wire racks. Eat warm or at room temperature.

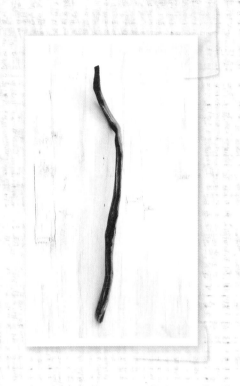

☞ **STYLING TIP**

Be inspired by nature when styling your table; pebbles, bark, feathers and flowers can all add a sense of fun.

CORN *and* BACON POLENTA 'MUFFINS'

MAKES 12 MUFFINS

Although I call these muffins, they're a bit of a cross between a muffin and a frittata. But one thing's for sure: they are definitely a must if there'll be kids at your gathering because they're really tasty and have no chilli or herby 'green bits' to cause complaints. However, if it's an adults-only affair, feel free to add some chopped coriander leaves, or a chopped green chilli, or both.

vegetable oil for greasing
1 corn on the cob (or 150 g frozen
    corn kernels, thawed)
2 teaspoons olive oil
125 g rindless bacon
150 g (1 cup) plain (all-purpose)
    flour
3 teaspoons baking powder
100 g (½ cup) polenta
3 free-range eggs, lightly beaten
200 ml milk
75 g butter, melted
35 g (⅓ cup) parmesan cheese,
    finely grated

1 Preheat fan-forced oven to 180°C (200°C conventional/ Gas 6) and grease a 12-hole (capacity 80 ml or ⅓ cup) muffin tin. If using corn on the cob, cook the corn in a saucepan of boiling salted water for 5 minutes. Leave to cool for 5 minutes, then carefully slice off the corn kernels with a sharp knife.

2 Meanwhile, heat the oil in a frying pan over medium heat and fry the bacon for about 5 minutes, until crisp. Drain on paper towel, cool slightly and then dice.

3 Sift the flour and baking powder into a large bowl then stir in the polenta. In a separate bowl or jug, combine the eggs, milk and melted butter and season well with sea salt and freshly ground black pepper.

4 Add the egg mixture to the flour mixture and gently combine. Then add the parmesan, corn and bacon and stir just to combine; do not overmix.

5 Spoon into the prepared muffin tin and bake for about 20 minutes, until the muffins have risen and are golden. Cool in the tin for 5 minutes then turn out onto wire racks to cool. Serve warm or at room temperature.

VERY QUICK FETA *and* HERB BREAD ROLLS

MAKES 8 ROLLS

This is a very quick, all-in-one bread recipe. To make the process quicker and easier, I use beer instead of yeast to make the rolls rise. These quite dense rolls are delicious eaten just with butter or with a ham or salami filling; they're also great with guacamole and hummus (see page 66).

450 g (3 cups) self-raising flour, plus about 2 tablespoons extra
1 teaspoon table salt
200 ml beer, at room temperature
2 tablespoons olive oil
100 g feta, crumbled
1½ teaspoons dried oregano

1 Combine all the ingredients in a large bowl and, using your hands, bring the mixture together. If it's a bit sticky, add the extra flour. Knead for about 10 minutes, until soft and elastic – this can be as simple as pushing and stretching the mixture in the bowl. Alternatively, transfer it to a floured surface for kneading.

2 Cover the mixture in the bowl with a clean tea towel and leave it in a warm place for 30 minutes, until the dough has risen and grown a little bit in size.

3 Preheat fan-forced oven to 170°C (190°C conventional/ Gas 5) and lightly flour a baking tray. Punch the centre of the risen bread, then divide it into eight equal portions (see tip). Form each portion into a ball and cut a cross on the top. Place on the floured tray, allowing a little room for expansion.

4 Bake for 20–30 minutes. The rolls should sound hollow when tapped. Carefully transfer from the tray onto a wire rack. Serve warm or cold.

5 If transporting the rolls, wrap them in a clean tea towel while still warm to help keep them warm for your arrival.

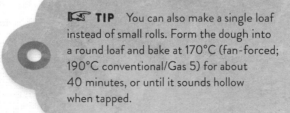

☞ **TIP** You can also make a single loaf instead of small rolls. Form the dough into a round loaf and bake at 170°C (fan-forced; 190°C conventional/Gas 5) for about 40 minutes, or until it sounds hollow when tapped.

PUMPKIN *and* CHEDDAR MUFFINS

MAKES 12 MUFFINS

These savoury muffins are usually a hit with kids and adults alike. The muffins last two to three days in an airtight container and can also be frozen, so they're perfect for lunchboxes too.

2 tablespoons olive oil,
   plus extra for greasing
500 g pumpkin flesh, cubed
1 teaspoon ground cumin
3 free-range eggs, lightly beaten
125 ml (½ cup) milk
60 ml (¼ cup) vegetable oil
225 g (1½ cups) self-raising flour
1 teaspoon table salt
100 g (1 cup) cheddar or tasty
   cheese, finely grated

1 Preheat fan-forced oven to 180°C (200°C conventional/Gas 6) and grease a 12-hole (capacity 80 ml or ⅓ cup) muffin tin. Put the olive oil into a baking dish and heat in the oven for 5–10 minutes.

2 Add the pumpkin to the baking dish, sprinkle with the cumin and season with sea salt and freshly ground black pepper. Shake the pan to coat the pumpkin in the seasoned oil. Roast for 25–30 minutes, shaking the pan once or twice during cooking. Once soft and starting to blacken a little in some places, remove from the oven and set aside. Reduce oven temperature to 170°C (190°C conventional/Gas 5).

3 Combine the eggs, milk and vegetable oil in a large bowl. Sift the flour and salt over the egg mixture and fold in gently to combine. Stir in the pumpkin and any pan juices, mashing the pumpkin slightly, then add the cheese.

4 Spoon the mixture into the muffin tin and bake for about 20 minutes, until the muffins have risen and are golden. Leave to cool in the tin for 5 minutes then transfer to wire racks to cool further. Serve warm or at room temperature.

☞ **STYLING TIP**
Individually wrap muffins with baking paper and tie with rustic string.

FLAKY
and
CRUMBLY

IS THERE ANYTHING better than a homemade pie? In this chapter you'll find a savoury pie or tart to suit pretty much everyone, from the very pretty individual summer vegetable tartlets, made with a delicious parmesan pastry, to the show-stopping chicken and pork picnic pie. And the tips on safe transportation ensure there's no need to worry that your dish won't make it to your destination in one piece.

Turning up to a gathering with a homemade pie or a selection of tartlets shows that you care and have taken the time with your offering.
Flaky pastry anyone?

SUMMER VEGETABLE TARTLETS

MAKES 6 TARTLETS

With a crumbly parmesan pastry crust and a creamy egg-custard filling, these tartlets are perfect for a summer picnic.

PASTRY
175 g plain (all-purpose) flour
75 g chilled butter, cubed
1 free-range egg yolk
25 g parmesan cheese, finely grated

FILLING
1 small zucchini (courgette)
200–250 g asparagus, cut into
   3 cm lengths
1 free-range egg, beaten
150 ml thickened cream
25 g parmesan cheese, finely grated

1 To make the pastry, put the flour into the bowl of a food processor. Add the butter and process for about 30 seconds, until all the butter is mixed in with the flour. Add the egg and parmesan and process again briefly, then add about 1½ tablespoons of water and process briefly again. Transfer to a bowl and form into a ball. Divide the pastry into six equal portions, then wrap each portion in plastic wrap and chill for 15 minutes.

2 After chilling, roll each portion out to about a 12 cm circle and use the circles to line six 8 cm tartlet tins. Trim the edges.

3 If it's a particularly warm day, chill the pastry-lined tartlet tins for 15 minutes in the fridge. Preheat fan-forced oven to 180°C (200°C conventional/Gas 6). Line each tartlet with baking paper and then weigh down with baking beans or raw rice. Bake for 10 minutes then remove the paper and weights and bake for a further 5 minutes. Set aside. Reduce the oven temperature to 170°C (190°C conventional/Gas 5).

4 Meanwhile, cut the zucchini in half lengthways then slice into ½ cm semicircles. Blanch the zucchini and asparagus in boiling water for 1 minute, then drain well and refresh under cold water. Drain well again.

5 Combine the egg, cream and two-thirds of the parmesan and season well with sea salt and freshly ground black pepper. Divide the vegetables between the tartlets then pour the egg mixture over the top, filling each tin to the top of the pastry edge. Scatter the remaining parmesan over the top. Bake for about 15 minutes, until the tartlets are just set and lightly golden on top (they'll continue to cook as they cool, so do not overcook). Cool in the tins on a wire rack.

6 Serve warm or cold. For ease of transportation, leave the tartlets in their tins.

CHICKEN *and* PORK PICNIC PIE

SERVES 8–10

This is a rich savoury pie, the kind we used to take on picnics in England. It's made up of layers of poached chicken, sausage meat and a bacon-and-sweet-corn stuffing, all encased in a delicious shortcrust pastry. For added flavour, I use sausage meat from sausages, rather than plain sausage meat.

500 g boneless, skinless chicken breast, preferably free range
400–500 g good-quality pork sausages
1 free-range egg, lightly beaten

PASTRY
400 g plain (all-purpose) flour
180 g chilled butter, cubed

STUFFING
2 teaspoons olive oil
75 g rindless bacon, diced
1 small onion, finely chopped
2 garlic cloves, crushed
100 g fresh breadcrumbs (from day-old bread)
3 tablespoons flat-leaf parsley, chopped
3 tablespoons basil leaves, chopped
1 cooked corn on the cob, kernels sliced off (or about 100 g frozen corn kernels, thawed)
1 free-range egg, beaten
25 g butter, melted

green salad to serve
chutney to serve

1 To make the pastry, put the flour and butter into a food processor and mix for about 30 seconds, until the mixture resembles fine breadcrumbs. Add 100 ml of cold water and process for 10 seconds. Transfer to a large bowl or work surface and form into a ball (adding a little more water if necessary), kneading very briefly. Divide the pastry into one-third and two-thirds. Press each portion into a disc and wrap in plastic wrap. Chill for 15 minutes.

2 Roll out the larger of the two pieces to 33–34 cm, or sufficient to line the base and side of a 20–21 cm springform (or loose-based) tin (depth 6–7 cm), allowing any excess pastry to hang over the sides. Chill until needed.

3 Slice the chicken breast in half horizontally. Put it into a saucepan and add just enough water to cover the chicken. Bring to the boil, then reduce the heat to a simmer and cook for 5 minutes. Remove from the heat and leave for 10 minutes. Drain the water and set aside (the chicken doesn't have to be cooked through).

4 To make the stuffing, heat the oil in a frying pan and fry the bacon for 3 minutes. Add the onion and garlic and fry for about 5 minutes until softened. Transfer to a bowl and leave to cool for 5 minutes. Stir in the breadcrumbs, parsley, basil, corn and beaten egg. Mix thoroughly, then season well with sea salt and freshly ground black pepper and stir in the butter.

5 Take half the stuffing and spread it over the pastry base, pressing it down gently with the back of a spoon. Shred the chicken and layer it on top.

6 Slit the skins of the sausages and put the meat into a bowl, squashing it all together, then spread it in a layer on top of the chicken, pressing it to the edges. Top with the remaining stuffing, once again gently pressing it down.

7 Preheat fan-forced oven to 180°C (200°C conventional/Gas 6). Roll out the remaining pastry to a circle about 22 cm across. With the excess pastry hanging over the edge, brush the top edge of the pastry in the tin with the beaten egg, then lift the lid onto the pie. Seal gently, pressing down with the tines of a fork. Trim the edges, ensuring the pie is well sealed. Brush the lid with beaten egg and cut a cross in the middle of the pastry to allow steam to escape.

8 Place the pie on a baking tray and bake for 50 minutes, then brush it with egg again (to get a glossy finish) and bake for a further 10 minutes. Leave to cool completely in the tin before slicing. If transporting the pie, leave it in the tin to keep it safe. Serve accompanied with a dressed green salad and chutney.

☞ STYLING TIP

It's fun to have one-off pieces of cutlery, so keep an eye out for interesting pieces to collect, like these different knives.

ROASTED RED CAPSICUM
and FETA TART

SERVES 6

Once you've made and eaten this tart, I wouldn't be surprised if it became one of your regular 'go-to' recipes.

PASTRY
230 g plain (all-purpose) flour
100 g chilled butter, cubed

FILLING
1 large red capsicum (pepper),
   halved and deseeded
   (or 100 g bought chargrilled
   capsicum, drained)
3 free-range eggs, lightly beaten
150 ml pouring cream
1 x quantity onion jam (page 50)
100 g feta, crumbled

1 To make the pastry, put the flour into the bowl of a food processor. Add the butter and process for about 30 seconds, or until all the butter is mixed in with the flour. Add 2½–3 tablespoons of water and process briefly. Transfer to a bowl and form into a ball. Flatten into a disc, wrap in plastic wrap and chill for 20 minutes.

2 Meanwhile, heat grill to high. Squash the capsicum halves flat, place under the hot grill and cook until the skin blackens and blisters. Put the capsicum into a plastic bag, seal the bag and leave for 15 minutes. Rub or peel off the skin (do not rinse) and slice the capsicum halves into thin strips 3–4 cm long.

3 Roll out the pastry and use it to line the base and side of a 23 cm flan tin. Chill for 15 minutes.

4 Preheat fan-forced oven to 170°C (190°C conventional/ Gas 5). After the pastry has chilled, line it with baking paper then weigh down with baking beans or raw rice. Bake for 20 minutes then remove the paper and weights and bake for a further 5 minutes or until the base is cooked through. Set aside.

5 Reduce the heat to 160°C (180°C conventional/Gas 4). Combine the eggs and cream and season well with sea salt and freshly ground black pepper. Spoon the onion jam onto the base of the cooked pastry and sprinkle the feta over the top. Pour the egg mixture over the top to just below the rim of the pastry, then scatter the strips of capsicum on top.

6 Bake for 20–25 minutes or until set and golden. Cool in the tin. If transporting, leave the tart whole in the tin to keep it safe. To serve, remove from the tin then slice.

ROASTED PUMPKIN, PARMESAN and HERB PASTIES

MAKES 12 PASTIES

These pasties are so delicious that one is rarely enough! For convenience they can be frozen uncooked and then cooked as required. If cooking from frozen, cook for an additional 5 minutes.

1 whole garlic bulb

2 tablespoons olive oil

300 g pumpkin flesh, diced

80 g (¾ cup) parmesan, grated

2 tablespoons flat-leaf parsley, finely chopped

2 tablespoons basil, shredded

3 sheets frozen puff pastry (about 24 x 24 cm), thawed in fridge

1 free-range egg, lightly beaten

1 tablespoon milk

1 tablespoon sesame or poppy seeds (optional)

chutney to serve (optional)

1 Heat fan-forced oven to 180°C (200°C conventional/ Gas 6). Wrap the garlic bulb in foil and place on a baking sheet. Roast for 50–60 minutes, or until it feels very soft.

2 At the same time, heat the oil in a roasting tin for 10 minutes. Add the pumpkin, season with sea salt and freshly ground black pepper and roast for 25–30 minutes or until soft and a few of the corners are starting to blacken. Set aside for 10 minutes to cool (leave the oven turned on).

3 When cool enough to handle, snip off the tops of the garlic cloves and squeeze the purée from each clove into a bowl. Add the parmesan, parsley and basil and season with sea salt and freshly ground black pepper. Add the cooled pumpkin and any pan juices. Combine.

4 Cut out four 10 cm circles from each sheet of pastry. Divide the pumpkin mixture between the circles, placing it onto one half of each circle only.

5 Combine the egg and milk then brush the edge of each circle. Fold over and gently seal, then press along the edges with the tines of a fork. Brush all over with the egg mixture and sprinkle with sesame seeds. Place on two or three lined baking sheets and bake for 20–25 minutes or until the pasties are puffed and golden. Serve warm or at room temperature, accompanied by chutney, if liked.

INDIVIDUAL EGG, BACON *and* SPINACH PIES

MAKES 12 PIES

These tasty little pies are a great way to get the breakfast favourites of egg and bacon together in one bite. Any leftovers (although I doubt there will be any) could be popped into a lunchbox for a treat.

3 sheets frozen puff pastry (about 24 x 24 cm), thawed in fridge

FILLING
2 teaspoons olive oil
125 g rindless smoked bacon, fat trimmed
120 g baby spinach leaves
3 free-range eggs
2 free-range egg yolks
150 ml pouring cream
2 tablespoons basil leaves, torn
3 tablespoons parmesan cheese, grated

1 Using a pastry cutter, cut out four 10 cm circles from each sheet of puff pastry (see tip). Roll them out to make them slightly thinner and bigger. Use the pastry circles to line a 12-hole (capacity 80 ml or ⅓ cup) muffin tin. Chill until needed. Preheat fan-forced oven to 180°C (200°C conventional/Gas 6).

2 Heat the oil in a frying pan and cook the bacon until crispy. Remove from the pan and dice.

3 Wash the spinach leaves, then put them into a saucepan with only the water from their wash clinging to their leaves (i.e. no additional water is required). Cover with a lid and cook over medium heat for about 1 minute, shaking the pan regularly, until the leaves are wilted. Drain and cool slightly then squeeze out the excess water. Finely chop.

4 Briefly whisk together the whole eggs and egg yolks. Measure out the cream in a jug and add the beaten eggs, basil and cheese. Season with sea salt and freshly ground black pepper and stir to combine.

5 Divide the spinach leaves between the pastry cases and top with the bacon. Carefully pour the egg mixture over the top. Bake for about 20–25 minutes until the filling is firm and the pastry is puffed and golden. Double-check the pastry bases are cooked.

6 Cool in the tin for 5 minutes then turn out to cool completely. Return the pies to the muffin tin for ease of transportation. If serving warm, keep the still-warm pies in the tin and wrap in a tea towel and transport immediately.

TIP If you don't have any pastry cutters, simply cut the pastry into quarters and use the squares to line the holes. Brush the pastry with beaten egg and bake for an extra 5 minutes to ensure the bases are fully cooked.

MUSHROOM VOL-AU-VENTS

MAKES 12 VOL-AU-VENTS

Yes, I know vol-au-vents are so 1970s, but although we may laugh, most of us secretly love them. These ones are particularly good, made with wild mushrooms and parmesan. It's time to bring back the vol-au-vent!

15 g dried wild mushrooms, such as chanterelles

4 sheets frozen puff pastry (about 24 x 24 cm), thawed in fridge

1 free-range egg, lightly beaten

20 g butter

2 tablespoons olive oil

1 garlic clove, crushed

200 g chestnut mushrooms, roughly chopped

1 tablespoon brandy or marsala (optional)

30 g (⅓ cup) parmesan cheese, finely grated

100 g crème fraîche

2 tablespoons flat-leaf parsley, finely chopped

☞ TIP

Don't waste the cut out circles: brush them with egg, sprinkle with a little sugar and bake for about 15 minutes. Serve topped with whipped cream and jam.

1 Soak the wild mushrooms in warm water for 30 minutes to soften.

2 Preheat fan-forced oven to 180°C (200°C conventional/ Gas 6). Using a 7 cm cutter, cut out nine circles from each sheet of pastry. Place 12 circles onto lined baking trays and brush with the egg. Brush half (12) of the remaining circles with egg also, and top each one with a second circle, to form a little stack.

3 Using a 5 cm cutter, cut out the centre from each double stack (see tip) and place the resulting double stack of rings on top of each of the 12 circles on the baking trays. Carefully brush the tops with egg, ensuring you don't brush the sides, as this may prevent the vol-au-vents from rising. If it's a hot day, chill the pastry in the fridge for 15 minutes. Bake for about 20 minutes, or until puffed and golden. Transfer to wire racks to cool.

4 Meanwhile, drain the mushrooms, reserving the soaking liquid, and roughly chop. Heat the butter and oil in a frying pan over medium heat, then add the garlic and fry gently for 1–2 minutes without browning. Add the chestnut and wild mushrooms and fry for 6–7 minutes or until their juices have evaporated.

5 Add 1 tablespoon of the mushroom-soaking liquid and the brandy, or an extra tablespoon of soaking liquid if not using alcohol. Increase the heat, stir well and cook until the liquid has almost evaporated. Remove from the heat and season with sea salt and plenty of freshly ground black pepper.

6 Combine the parmesan, crème fraîche and parsley, then gently fold through the mushrooms. Divide the mushroom filling between the pastry shells and serve.

7 If transporting, keep the shells and filling separate, then fill the shells on arrival to prevent the pastry becoming soggy.

☞ **STYLING TIP**

Typography can be used in a multitude of fun ways when planning your table setting or picnic.

FILO PASTRY TARTLETS *with* ROASTED TOMATO, CAPSICUM *and* BASIL

MAKES 12 TARTLETS

These delicate tartlets are ideal for a summer picnic or tea in the garden. I suggest buying fresh filo pastry, as you won't need the whole packet so any leftover pastry can be frozen.

1 large red capsicum (pepper),
   halved and deseeded
   (or 100 g bought chargrilled
   capsicum, drained)
3 tablespoons olive oil
24 cherry tomatoes
1 garlic clove, crushed
3 tablespoons panko
   (Japanese breadcrumbs)
   or fresh breadcrumbs
   (from day-old bread)
60 g butter, melted
6 sheets filo pastry
200–250 g crème fraîche
3 tablespoons basil leaves,
   finely shredded, plus 12 small
   basil leaves

1 Heat grill to high. Squash the capsicum flat then grill it until the skin blackens and blisters. Put it into a plastic bag, seal the bag and leave for 15 minutes. Rub or peel off the skin (do not rinse). Slice into thin strips 3–4 cm long. Set aside.

2 Preheat fan-forced oven to 180°C (200°C conventional/ Gas 6). Put 2 tablespoons of the oil into a baking dish and put into the oven to heat up. Once hot, add the tomatoes and season well with sea salt and freshly ground black pepper. Roast for about 20 minutes, or until the tomatoes start to soften and blacken in a few places.

3 Meanwhile, heat the remaining tablespoon of oil in a frying pan and add the garlic. Fry gently for 1 minute without browning. Add the panko, season with sea salt and freshly ground black pepper and fry for about 2 minutes until golden. Transfer to paper towel to cool.

4 Brush a 12-hole (capacity 80 ml or ⅓ cup) muffin tin with melted butter. Keep the filo pastry covered to prevent it drying out, then take a sheet and fold it three times, until you have a square of approximately 11 cm. Cut along the seams to make individual squares. Repeat until you have 48 squares, covering them as you cut them.

5 Brush a square with melted butter then place a second square on top to form a star shape. Brush with melted butter again and repeat with two more pieces of pastry, so you have a stack of four squares of pastry. Place the pastry stack into one of the muffin-tin holes, pushing down gently to line the hole and flatten the base, ensuring there are no air bubbles in the base. Repeat to fill all the holes.

6 Bake for about 10 minutes or until golden brown. Remove to a wire rack to cool. If any of the bases have risen, gently break the pastry but make sure you don't put a hole in the bottom.

7 Put the crème fraîche into a bowl, stir in the shredded basil and season with sea salt and freshly ground black pepper. Divide the mixture between the tartlet shells, then top with a few strips of roasted capsicum and two cherry tomatoes. Scatter the garlic breadcrumbs over the tomatoes and top with a basil leaf.

8 If transporting, return the pastry shells to the tin before filling.

TOMATO *and* SHALLOT SAVOURY TARTE TATIN

SERVES 6–8

Tarte tatin is often associated with dessert, but savoury versions are delicious too and this one is no exception.

250 g French shallots, unpeeled
1 tablespoon olive oil
25 g butter
2 garlic cloves, crushed
6 roma tomatoes,
   halved lengthways
1 tablespoon thyme leaves,
   plus extra to garnish
1 teaspoon sugar
1 sheet frozen puff pastry (about
   24 x 24 cm), thawed in fridge

1 Find yourself a 20 cm (across the base) ovenproof frying pan. Check the handle is ovenproof too, i.e. not plastic, or cover it with a double layer of foil. Also check it fits in your oven with the door closed! Preheat fan-forced oven to 180°C (200°C conventional/Gas 6).

2 Simmer the shallots in water for 5 minutes, then drain well. Cool slightly then peel (the skins should slip off easily).

3 Heat the oil in your frying pan. Add the shallots and cook for about 5 minutes or until starting to brown. Transfer to a plate and remove the oil from the pan.

4 Put the butter in the pan over low heat. Once it has melted, add the garlic and stir around briefly. Add the tomatoes cut-side down and sprinkle with the thyme and sugar. Cook over medium heat for 1 minute. Remove from the heat and add the shallots, ensuring that everything is in a single, compact layer.

5 If your pastry is a square sheet, snip off the corners to make them rounded. Carefully place the pastry over the shallots, tucking it inside the pan (not over the edges of the pan).

6 Place on a baking sheet and bake for 30–35 minutes until the pastry is puffed and golden. Remove from the oven and cool in the pan for 5 minutes. Then carefully turn out onto a large serving plate, remembering the handle will still be hot. Also be aware the tomatoes may have leaked a little juice. Serve warm or cold, scattered with the extra thyme.

7 If transporting, cover with foil once cool.

Mini
MORSELS

———————◆———————

WHETHER YOU'VE BEEN invited to a drinks party, an
afternoon garden tea or a picnic in the park, in this chapter
you'll find a suitable (and delicious) answer to the 'bring
a plate' question. All the dishes are one- or two-bite finger
food, and most of them don't require cutlery – just provide
a stack of pretty napkins and away you go.

Choose from sesame-crusted tuna with wasabi
mayonnaise dip, prawn cakes with cucumber dipping
sauce, crowd-pleasing mini meatballs or one of
the other simple, lip-smacking bites.

SMOKY CORN *and* AVOCADO MEXICAN BITES

MAKES SUFFICIENT TOPPING FOR 30–35 ROUND TORTILLA CHIPS

Sometimes the simplest ideas are the best. These came to me when I had to quickly pull something together for a group of friends who came round at late notice. Round tortilla chips make a better platform for the topping, but this recipe will work with triangular ones as well, although you'd probably use less filling on each.

1 corn cob, husk removed

olive oil, for brushing

2 tomatoes

1 avocado, diced

2 tablespoons coriander,
   finely chopped

1 tablespoon lime juice

1 red chilli, deseeded and
   finely chopped

30–35 round tortilla chips

1 lime, cut into wedges, to serve

1 Cook the corn in boiling water for 5 minutes. Drain the corn and let it sit for 2–3 minutes. Heat a chargrill pan over medium–high heat. Brush the corn all over with the oil and chargrill for 10–15 minutes, turning it regularly until it's chargrilled in several places. Allow it to cool slightly, then slice off the kernels using a sharp knife.

2 Quarter the tomatoes then scoop out the seeds. Dice the flesh and put it into a bowl with the corn kernels, avocado, coriander, lime juice and chilli. Combine gently.

3 Arrange the corn chips in a single layer on a serving plate and top each one with a spoonful of filling. Serve with lime wedges.

4 If transporting, top the tortilla chips on arrival.

☞ STYLING TIP

Stacks of paper napkins are notorious for flying away when eating outside. Pop an interesting stone on top to weigh them down.

MINI PROSCIUTTO *and* GOATS CHEESE 'TARTLETS'

MAKES 12 TARTLETS

Although I call these tartlets, they are simpler than a traditional tartlet because you don't need to worry about pastry or tartlet tins. The shell is made of thin strips of prosciutto and the 'tartlets' are cooked in a muffin tin.

6 asparagus spears
olive oil, for greasing
160 g prosciutto, thinly sliced
80 g goats cheese or Persian feta, crumbled
2 free-range eggs, beaten
200 ml thick (double/heavy) cream

1 Preheat fan-forced oven to 160°C (180°C conventional/ Gas 4). Snap off and discard the woody ends of the asparagus. Slice the stalks into 1 cm pieces. Blanch in boiling salted water for 1 minute. Drain and refresh under cold water then drain again.

2 Grease a 12-hole (approximate capacity 40 ml) patty pan. Line the base and sides of the holes with the prosciutto, ensuring there are no holes or gaps.

3 Divide the goats cheese and half the asparagus between the shells. Combine the eggs and cream and season well with sea salt and freshly ground black pepper. Carefully pour into the patty pan holes. Top with the remaining asparagus.

4 Bake for 18–20 minutes or until the tartlets are puffed and golden. Cool in the tin for 10 minutes then transfer to a wire rack to cool. Serve warm or at room temperature.

5 If transporting a while after cooking, it's best to cool the tartlets completely then return them to the tin for transporting. Or transport them warm in the tin.

☞ **STYLING TIP**
Serve sea salt flakes, ground pepper and other condiments in vintage bakeware.

CROSTINI

MAKES ABOUT 30 CROSTINI

Crostini are always a party pleaser. Don't be tempted to make the crostini bases more than 24 hours in advance, otherwise they'll have the texture of cardboard! The recipe for each topping is enough to cover half the crostini; if you only want to make one topping, simply double its ingredients.

1 medium day-old baguette
  or loaf of day-old ciabatta
100 ml olive oil

ROASTED CAPSICUM AND GOATS CHEESE TOPPING

1 red capsicum (pepper), halved
  and deseeded (or 75 g bought
  chargrilled capsicum, drained)
2 teaspoons olive oil
2 teaspoons sherry vinegar or white
  wine vinegar
2 tablespoons basil leaves, torn
50 g goats cheese

ONION JAM AND BRIE TOPPING

2 tablespoons olive oil
2 large onions, thinly sliced
½ teaspoon sea salt
1 tablespoon brown sugar
1 tablespoon balsamic vinegar
1 tablespoon thyme leaves,
  roughly chopped
100 g brie

1 Preheat fan-forced oven to 170°C (190°C conventional/ Gas 5). To make the crostini, slice the baguette into 1 cm thick slices (if using ciabatta, slice each piece into quarters). Brush both sides with olive oil, season with sea salt and freshly ground black pepper and toast in the oven for about 10 minutes until just crisp. Set aside to cool. If making the toasts a day in advance, store in an airtight container.

2 Heat grill to high. To make the capsicum topping, squash the capsicum flat, then grill it until the skin blackens and blisters. Put it into a plastic bag, seal the bag and leave for 15 minutes, then rub or peel off the skin (do not rinse). Slice the capsicum into thin strips 3–4 cm long, then put it into a bowl with the olive oil, sherry vinegar and basil, seasoning well with sea salt and freshly ground black pepper. Stir to mix everything well then set aside.

3 To make the onion jam, heat the oil in a medium saucepan, add the onion and sea salt and stir to coat the onion well. Cover and cook over medium heat for 15 minutes, stirring occasionally, until the onions start to go golden brown. Reduce the heat and cook for a further 15 minutes, still covered. Add the sugar and vinegar, stirring well and scraping up any bits stuck on the bottom of the pan, and cook for a final 15 minutes. Stir in the thyme then set aside to cool.

4 If transporting, take the crostini and toppings in separate containers and assemble on arrival. Top half the crostini with the roasted capsicum topping and small bits of goats cheese. Divide the onion jam between the remaining crostini, then top each one with a small piece of gooey brie.

OYSTERS *with* ASIAN DRESSING

MAKES 12 OYSTERS

You wouldn't want to be taking these with you on a long hike or storing them in the back of a hot car, but these simple and very delicious morsels are ideal for lunch in the garden or at a friend's house. The dressing can easily be doubled to serve more.

12 of your favourite oysters,
  on the shell
crushed ice or plenty of rock salt
  to serve (optional)
12 coriander leaves to garnish

DRESSING
1 tablespoon lime juice
1 tablespoon fish sauce
1 teaspoon sesame oil
1 teaspoon rice vinegar
1 teaspoon sugar
1 small red chilli, deseeded
  and finely chopped

1   Combine the lime juice, fish sauce, sesame oil, rice vinegar, sugar and chilli, stirring well to dissolve the sugar.

2   Create a bed of crushed ice or rock salt on a serving platter and arrange the oysters on top.

3   Spoon a little dressing onto each oyster and garnish with a coriander leaf. Serve immediately.

4   If taking the oysters to a friend's house, sit them on ice packs in an esky (cool box) to keep them cool while in transit, and transport the dressing in an airtight container. Put the oysters into the fridge as soon as you arrive at your destination.

☞ **STYLING TIP**
Use old or new Scrabble letters to personalise your table.

PRAWN CAKES *with* CUCUMBER DIPPING SAUCE

MAKES 16 PRAWN CAKES

These prawn cakes are delicious eaten hot or cold. If going on a picnic, chill them before leaving and keep them chilled until it's time to eat. For a barbecue, take them raw and cook them on-site, serving them hot. You could also try wrapping them in lettuce leaves to serve.

500 g raw prawns,
    peeled and deveined
2 teaspoons lemongrass,
    finely chopped
3 makrut (kaffir) lime leaves,
    finely chopped
1 small red or green chilli,
    deseeded and finely chopped
2 teaspoons lime juice
2 teaspoons fish sauce
1 free-range egg white
2 tablespoons coriander leaves,
    chopped
2 tablespoons mint leaves, chopped
40 g (⅔ cup) panko
    (Japanese breadcrumbs)
vegetable oil, for grilling

CUCUMBER DIPPING SAUCE

2 tablespoons caster sugar
1 small Lebanese cucumber
1 small red shallot or French shallot,
    thinly sliced
1 small red chilli, sliced into
    thin rings
1 tablespoon rice vinegar

1 Put the prawns into the bowl of a food processor and pulse for about 10 seconds until roughly chopped. Add the lemongrass, lime leaves, chilli, lime juice, fish sauce, egg white, coriander and mint leaves and pulse for about 10 seconds more, or until just combined. Do not over-process.

2 Transfer to a bowl and stir in the panko. Slightly wet your hands to make handling the mixture easier, then form into about 16 small patty shapes, about 5 cm round. Put the patties in a single layer on a plate and chill in the fridge for 30 minutes.

3 Meanwhile, make the dipping sauce. Put the caster sugar into a small bowl with a large pinch of salt and add 2 tablespoons of hot water, stirring to dissolve the sugar. Leave to cool.

4 Peel the cucumber, halve it lengthways, scrape out the seeds using a teaspoon, then dice. Divide the cucumber, shallot and chilli between a couple of small serving dishes. Stir the vinegar into the cooled sugar liquid then pour this liquid over the vegetables.

5 Heat a chargrill pan over medium heat. Brush the prawn patties lightly with vegetable oil and cook for about 2–3 minutes on each side, until they're lightly browned and cooked through. Drain on paper towel. They can be eaten hot, warm or cold accompanied by the dipping sauce.

6 If transporting, arrange the prawn cakes in single layers between sheets of baking paper. Take the dressing in an airtight container.

☞ STYLING TIP

Look for vintage glassware in second-hand shops and at markets, and use it to add some sparkle to your table.

MINI MEATBALLS *with* HERB DIPPING SAUCE

MAKES ABOUT 40 MEATBALLS

Meatballs are a favourite with the young and old alike. I like to make lots of little one-bite balls, but you can make them bigger if you prefer. The dipping sauce is a delicious accompaniment, although you might find your younger guests munching on just the meatballs!

3–4 tablespoons olive oil
1 small red onion, finely chopped
3 garlic cloves, crushed
1 or 2 tablespoons harissa paste
1 kg lamb mince
2 tablespoons flat-leaf parsley, finely chopped
2 tablespoons mint, finely chopped
finely grated zest of 1 lemon
30 g (½ cup) panko (Japanese breadcrumbs)

HERB DIPPING SAUCE
80 ml (⅓ cup) olive oil
2 tablespoons lemon juice
4 tablespoons coriander leaves, finely chopped
4 tablespoons flat-leaf parsley, finely chopped
2 garlic cloves, crushed

1 Heat 1 tablespoon of the oil in a frying pan and gently fry the onion and garlic for about 5 minutes, without browning. Transfer to a large bowl and add the remaining meatball ingredients (except for the remaining olive oil). Season well with sea salt and freshly ground black pepper. Mix with your hands for about 2 minutes, or until the mixture turns a slightly paler pink.

2 Form the meatball mixture into about 40 small balls, each the size of a walnut (or larger if you prefer). Chill in the fridge for 30 minutes.

3 Meanwhile, make the dipping sauce. Whisk the oil and lemon juice together then stir through the remaining ingredients.

4 Heat 1–2 tablespoons of oil in a large frying pan and fry the meatballs in batches, adding a little extra oil if necessary; do not overcrowd the pan. Allow the meatballs to form a crust before turning. Cook for about 10 minutes or until browned all over and cooked through.

5 Cool the meatballs, then transport them and the sauce separately. Offer toothpicks to serve, if preferred.

SESAME-CRUSTED TUNA *with* WASABI MAYONNAISE DIP

SERVES 6

Make sure you don't overcook the tuna in this recipe, as the cubes will continue to cook as they cool. Wasabi is deceptively fiery, so don't be tempted to add too much and ensure it is well stirred into the mayonnaise.

3 (about 700 g) fresh tuna steaks
about 125 ml (½ cup) olive oil
100 g sesame seeds, mix of black
  and white
½–1 teaspoon freshly ground
  black pepper

WASABI MAYONNAISE
½–1 teaspoon wasabi
185 g (¾ cup) Japanese mayonnaise
  or good-quality egg mayonnaise
1 teaspoon mirin (available from
  the Asian section in most
  supermarkets)
1 teaspoon soy sauce
1 teaspoon rice vinegar or white
  wine vinegar

1 Cut each tuna steak into 2 cm cubes. Put about 2 tablespoons of the oil into a shallow dish. Add half the tuna cubes and toss gently to coat.

2 Put half the sesame seeds into a separate shallow dish and add half the black pepper. Roll the tuna cubes in the seed mixture, until they are completely coated. Repeat with the remaining tuna, sesame seeds and pepper (still using the original oil).

3 Heat about ½ cm of oil in a medium, heavy-based frying pan over medium–high heat. Fry the tuna cubes in batches (do not overcrowd the pan) for about 1½ minutes, turning them regularly. They should still be pink in the middle, and remember they'll continue to cook while cooling. Drain on paper towel and leave to cool.

4 To make the wasabi mayonnaise, put the wasabi in a bowl and gradually whisk in the mayonnaise, followed by the remaining ingredients.

5 If transporting, layer the cubes of tuna between pieces of baking paper and transport the wasabi mayo in an airtight container. Stick a toothpick into each tuna cube to serve (see tip).

☞ **TIP** Party-ware stores and Asian stores often stock fun toothpicks or mini skewers; pick up a packet when you see them.

SMOKED SALMON *and* ROASTED RED CAPSICUM PÂTÉ ON TOAST

SERVES 6

This creamy smoked salmon pâté served on crisp toast triangles is perfect finger food. You can make the pâté smooth or slightly chunky, depending on whether you blend the capsicum into the mix. If you stir the capsicum through after blending, the resulting pâté will be a little creamier.

1 small red capsicum (pepper),
    halved and deseeded (or 50 g
    bought chargrilled capsicum,
    drained)
200 g smoked salmon
200 g cream cheese
100 g sour cream
4 tablespoons dill, finely chopped
3–4 tablespoons lemon juice
8 thin slices of wholemeal bread

1 Preheat grill to high. Squash the capsicum halves to flatten them, then put them under the hot grill, skin side up. Grill until the skin is completely blackened. Transfer the capsicum to a plastic bag, seal the bag and leave for 15 minutes. Peel off the skin and finely dice the capsicum.

2 Put the smoked salmon, cream cheese, sour cream, dill and 3 tablespoons of the lemon juice into the bowl of a food processor and blend for about 20 seconds. Taste, then season with sea salt and freshly ground black pepper and add the extra tablespoon of lemon juice if needed. Then either add the diced capsicum and blend for 10 seconds or transfer the pâté to a bowl and stir in the diced capsicum. Put the mixture into the fridge for about 30 minutes to allow it to firm up slightly.

3 Heat fan-forced oven to 180°C (200°C conventional/ Gas 6) and put a baking sheet into the oven to heat up. Remove the crusts from the bread, then roll it out thinly using a rolling pin or bottle. Cut each piece into four triangles. Bake for 8–10 minutes until the toast is golden and crisp. Set aside to cool.

4 Store and transport the toast in an airtight container, then serve alongside the pâté.

☞ STYLING TIP

Invest in a set of alphabet stamps to personalise napkins, place settings, luggage tags and the like whenever you want.

Fresh and LEAFY

WHETHER IT'S A SIDE SALAD to accompany a selection of dishes or a substantial salad to serve as the main dish, this chapter has it covered. The quinoa salad with goats cheese, basil and crispy prosciutto is a filling, richly flavoured salad, while the dressed lettuce wedges make a nice change from your everyday green salad. The vegetable sticks in paper cups are ideal for a garden party or kid's birthday party, and the individual Thai beef salads are fun to serve on a picnic.

With transportation tips thrown in, you'll never serve a soggy salad again.

QUINOA SALAD *with* GOATS CHEESE, BASIL *and* CRISPY PROSCIUTTO

SERVES 4

This is a rich, indulgent salad, full of big flavours. You can replace the goats cheese with feta or a more mildly flavoured bocconcini if you prefer.

150 g (¾ cup) quinoa
3 tablespoons olive oil
2 tablespoons sherry vinegar
   or white wine vinegar
3 tablespoons small capers,
   rinsed and finely chopped
100 g prosciutto
handful basil leaves, larger leaves
   roughly torn
½ bunch watercress, leaves picked
150 g goats cheese, broken into
   small pieces

1 Bring 375 ml (1½ cups) of water to the boil in a medium saucepan. Add the quinoa, cover and return to the boil. Reduce the heat and simmer, covered, for 15 minutes until all of the water has been absorbed. Remove from the heat and place a clean tea towel over the saucepan, putting the lid on top of the tea towel – this helps any remaining moisture to be absorbed. Leave for 10 minutes.

2 Put the quinoa in a lidded bowl and add 2 tablespoons of the oil, the sherry vinegar and capers, and season well with sea salt and freshly ground black pepper. Toss to combine, then set aside to cool to room temperature.

3 Heat the remaining tablespoon of oil in a frying pan over medium–high heat. Add the prosciutto and fry for 2–3 minutes, until crispy. Remove the prosciutto from the pan (keeping the oil in the pan) and cool for a couple of minutes, then chop it into bite-sized pieces. Pour any oil from the pan over the quinoa mixture.

4 Add the prosciutto and basil to the quinoa and toss gently to combine. Sprinkle the watercress and pieces of goats cheese over the top. Put the lid on to transport.

5 Toss the watercress and goats cheese through the salad just before serving.

☞ **STYLING TIP**

You don't always have to take melamine or plastic on a picnic: add some vintage glamour with grandma's old cutlery.

VEGETABLE STICKS *in* PAPER CUPS

MAKES 8 SMALL CUPS

These are a great way to get kids (and adults) to eat vegetables while out and about, and they're also ideal for kids' birthday parties. You can vary the vegetables you use, depending on who you're catering for. You can also theme the cups to your occasion – I'm pretty sure Superman ate a lot of vegetables to be as super as he is.

As each cup has its own vegetable sticks and dip, the problem of double dipping is solved! Ensure your vegetable sticks are long enough to stick out the tops of the cups, or buy small cups.

2 carrots, cut into thin batons
2 cucumbers, cut into thin batons
8 radishes, halved (leave a leaf on
    if serving to adults)
1 small red capsicum (pepper),
    deseeded and cut into thin batons
1 small yellow capsicum (pepper),
    deseeded and cut into thin batons
2 celery stalks, cut into thin batons
24 snow peas (mangetout),
    cut into 3 lengthways
8 red or yellow cherry tomatoes,
    halved

GUACAMOLE
1 avocado, roughly chopped
1 red chilli, deseeded and finely
    chopped (optional)
1 tablespoon coriander,
    roughly chopped
1–2 tablespoons lime juice, to taste

HUMMUS
400 g tinned chickpeas, drained,
    rinsed and drained again
2 garlic cloves, crushed
½ teaspoon salt
2 tablespoons lemon juice
80–100 ml olive oil

1 To make the guacamole, combine the avocado, chilli and coriander in a bowl, season with a little sea salt and mash slightly. Add as little or as much lime juice as you like, probably depending on whether you're serving kids or adults.

2 To make the hummus, put the chickpeas, garlic and salt in a food processor and blend for about 5 seconds. Add the lemon juice, then start adding the oil and blend until you have the consistency you like, adding more oil if preferred.

3 Arrange your choice of vegetable sticks in your cups, then top each one with a tablespoon or two of the dips, serving any remaining dip on the side.

☞ STYLING TIP   If serving these for a child's birthday party, I also buy large noodle takeaway boxes, usually available cheaply from discount shops. I then arrange a couple of sandwich squares, the vegetable stick cups, and a small bunch of grapes or strawberries in each box, then hand each child their individual birthday tea. I have always found that kids will eat more when presented with food in this way rather than on platters. Obviously birthday cake and other goodies come after!

DRESSED LETTUCE WEDGES

SERVES 4–6

This is a really simple idea: instead of separating lettuce leaves and tossing in a dressing, serve wedges of crunchy baby cos with your choice of dressing. Try to buy baby cos lettuce as it looks prettier. It's up to you whether you make one, two or all three of the dressings.

4 baby cos lettuces, outer leaves discarded

BLACK OLIVE AND CAPER DRESSING

50 g pitted kalamata olives, chopped

1 tablespoon capers, drained, rinsed and drained again

2 tablespoons olive oil

1 teaspoon lemon rind, finely grated

small handful flat-leaf parsley, finely chopped

CUCUMBER AND BLACK VINEGAR DRESSING

1 tablespoon Chinese black vinegar (see tip)

1 teaspoon sesame oil

2 tablespoons lightly flavoured olive oil

2 small spring onions, finely chopped

½ Lebanese cucumber, finely diced

CREAMY LEMON AND HERB MAYONNAISE DRESSING

1 garlic clove, crushed

½ teaspoon salt

1 free-range egg yolk

125 ml (½ cup) light-flavoured olive oil

1 teaspoon dijon mustard

2 teaspoons lemon juice

1 tablespoon dill, finely chopped

1 tablespoon flat-leaf parsley, finely chopped

1 To make the black olive and caper dressing, put all the ingredients into a small blender or food processor and blend for 20–30 seconds; the dressing should still have some texture. If you don't have a small blender, finely chop the olives and capers and combine thoroughly with the other ingredients. Transfer to a bowl with a lid.

2 To make the cucumber and black vinegar dressing, put the vinegar, sesame oil, olive oil and spring onions into a small blender and blend until well combined. Transfer to a bowl with a lid and stir in the cucumber. If you don't have a small blender, put the ingredients into a jar with a lid and shake very well to ensure the oils and vinegar have combined. Then add the cucumber.

3 To make the mayonnaise dressing, put the garlic into a medium bowl with the salt. Using the back of a fork, mash the garlic and salt together until a really creamy paste forms. Add the egg yolk and, using an electric hand mixer, mix for 30 seconds. With the mixer in motion, start adding the oil, drop by drop – don't be tempted to add it faster, otherwise the mayonnaise may split. Once the mixture becomes thick and creamy you can add the oil in a steady stream. Add the mustard and lemon juice, continuing with the hand mixer, and check the seasoning, adding extra salt if needed. Stir in the dill and parsley and transfer to a lidded container. Put in the fridge until needed.

4 To serve, cut each lettuce in half lengthways, then cut each half into three wedges and arrange on a serving plate. Spoon some dressing onto each wedge, serving extra on the side. Alternatively serve the wedges and dressing separately, allowing guests to choose their own dressing.

5 If transporting, cut the lettuces, then reassemble them and wrap them in damp paper towel to both hold them together and keep them moist. Transport the three dressings separately. Serve as above.

TIP Find Chinese black vinegar in Asian grocery stores. Alternatively, you could substitute rice vinegar or white wine vinegar. You'll end up with a very different dressing, but it will still taste great!

PRAWN COCKTAIL *in a* JAR

SERVES 4

Serving food in jars has become very popular, but it's also a practical way of transporting a salad. To keep the jars safe while on the move, wrap each one in a large cloth napkin and present each person with a still-wrapped jar. You'll need four large, clean jars with lids.

20 medium raw king prawns,
   peeled and deveined,
   or 20 cooked prawns,
   peeled and deveined
150 g mixed salad leaves
paprika to dust

lemon wedges to serve

DRESSING
40 g (⅓ cup) good-quality
   egg mayonnaise
2 tablespoons sour cream
2 heaped teaspoons tomato sauce
dash of worcestershire sauce
couple of good shakes of
   Tabasco sauce
2 tablespoons lemon juice

1 I much prefer to buy raw prawns and cook them myself, but you can use cooked prawns. If using raw prawns, cook them in boiling water for about 3 minutes, or until they turn pink. Refresh under cold water. Cut each prawn into bite-sized pieces.

2 Combine all the dressing ingredients, adding extra lemon juice, Tabasco or worcestershire sauce as desired, to make a full-flavoured, tangy sauce.

3 Divide half the salad leaves among the jars (see tip), then add half the prawns. Top with the remaining salad leaves and remaining prawns. Put a spoonful or two of dressing on top of the seafood and sprinkle with paprika. Pop on the lids and screw tight.

4 If not transporting immediately, place the jars in the fridge until needed. To transport, wrap each jar in a large cloth napkin and secure with twine or a rubber band, tucking a fork into the side of each. Give guests their salad and suggest they mix the sauce into the salad before starting to eat. Offer the lemon wedges for squeezing over the salad.

TIP If you don't have any jars, you can, of course, serve the salad on a platter with the dressing spooned over.

LITTLE THAI BEEF *and* NOODLE SALADS TO GO

SERVES 6

This salad looks great served in cardboard takeaway noodle boxes. Fill the boxes before you leave home, then hand them out at mealtime. For a bit of fun, offer chopsticks or look out for bamboo cutlery.

3 makrut (kaffir) lime leaves
5 cm piece lemongrass,
    roughly chopped
1 garlic clove, chopped
5 cm piece ginger, finely grated
2 teaspoons vegetable oil
1 teaspoon fish sauce
700–800 g beef scotch fillet
1 tablespoon olive oil
375 g medium rice-stick noodles
250 g cherry tomatoes, quartered
1 small red onion, halved and
    thinly sliced
1 bunch coriander, leaves picked
1 bunch Thai basil or mint,
    leaves picked

CHILLI-LIME DRESSING
3 makrut (kaffir) lime leaves
4 tablespoons lime juice
2½ tablespoons fish sauce
3 teaspoons vegetable oil
1½ teaspoons sugar
1 small red chilli, deseeded
    and finely chopped

1 Thinly shred the makrut lime leaves and put into a spice grinder or small food processor with the lemongrass, garlic, ginger, vegetable oil and fish sauce. Grind to a paste. Rub the paste all over the beef and set the beef aside in the fridge for at least 1 hour or up to 4 hours.

2 Heat a chargrill pan over medium–high heat. Brush the beef with the olive oil and chargrill for 3–4 minutes on each side, until medium–rare, or until cooked to your liking, bearing in mind that it will continue to cook as it cools. Cover with foil and set aside for 10 minutes. Slice very thinly against the grain.

3 Meanwhile, cook the rice-stick noodles according to the packet instructions. Rinse under cold water, drain well and set aside.

4 To make the dressing, thinly shred the remaining lime leaves and combine them with the other dressing ingredients in a small bowl. Pour about three-quarters of the dressing over the noodles and toss well, then leave to cool completely.

5 If serving in noodle boxes, divide the noodles between six boxes (you may need to loosen them a bit using a couple of forks) and top with the cherry tomatoes, onion, herbs and beef. Alternatively put the noodles in a leak-proof container and top with the remaining ingredients. Take the remaining dressing in a separate container.

6 Serve the salad with a little extra dressing spooned over the top, mixing the salad gently as you eat.

☞ **STYLING TIP**
Buy bamboo cutlery then jazz
it up with some washi tape
(like very pretty masking tape),
available from craft stores.

ASIAN CRISPY COLESLAW

SERVES 6

This coleslaw is a great accompaniment to grilled fish and chicken. It's also delicious in burgers and sliders.

¼ (about 350 g) white cabbage
¼ (about 350 g) red cabbage
100 g snow peas (mangetout),
   shredded
1 red chilli, seeded and
   finely chopped
handful coriander leaves
handful mint leaves,
   larger leaves torn
2 tablespoons olive oil
2 tablespoons fish sauce
2 tablespoons lime juice
½ teaspoon sesame oil
½ teaspoon sugar
2 nashi pears, cored, halved and
   thinly sliced (optional; see tip)

1 Discard any discoloured outer leaves from the cabbages and remove the core. Shred both cabbages and put them into a bowl with the snow peas, chilli, coriander and mint. Toss to combine.

2 Combine the olive oil, fish sauce, lime juice, sesame oil and sugar.

3 Just before serving the salad, add the nashi pears to it. Pour the dressing over the top and toss to combine.

4 If taking the coleslaw on a picnic, transport the dressing in a separate container so the cabbages don't become soggy. To prevent the nashi pears browning during transport, either transport them whole and thinly slice on arrival, or put them in a container and squeeze a little lemon or lime juice over them.

TIP Nashi pears are very juicy, with a crisp, slightly grainy texture. They don't need to be peeled.

GREMOLATA CHICKEN, ASPARAGUS and COUSCOUS SALAD

SERVES 4–6

Gremolata is a delicious combination of flavours, most frequently used as a topping for the Italian dish osso bucco, but it's also great with a host of other dishes. Here I've made it into more of a dressing to coat tender poached chicken and steamed asparagus.

600–800 g boneless, skinless chicken breast (see tip), preferably free range
4 tablespoons olive oil
½ teaspoon table salt
300 g (1½ cups) couscous
juice of 1 lemon
200 300 g asparagus

GREMOLATA DRESSING
finely grated zest and juice of 1 lemon
1 small bunch flat-leaf parsley, finely chopped
1 large garlic clove, crushed
4 tablespoons olive oil

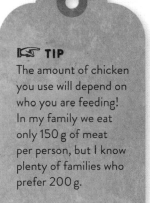

☞ TIP
The amount of chicken you use will depend on who you are feeding! In my family we eat only 150 g of meat per person, but I know plenty of families who prefer 200 g.

1 Make the gremolata first to allow the flavours to develop for a while. Combine the lemon zest (but not the juice) with the remaining dressing ingredients and season with sea salt and freshly ground black pepper.

2 Put the chicken in a medium saucepan and just cover with water; throw in a few parsley stalks from the parsley, too, if you have them. Bring to the boil. Reduce the heat to very low and simmer gently for 5 minutes. Remove from the heat and leave the chicken in the water to cool and finish cooking. Once the chicken is cooked through, remove it from the water and shred it into a bowl. Add the gremolata and toss to coat the chicken well. Set aside in the fridge until needed.

3 Meanwhile, bring 375 ml (1½ cups) of water, 2 tablespoons of the oil and the salt to the boil in a saucepan. Add the couscous, remove from the heat and fork through the grains to separate them. Cover and leave to stand for 2 minutes. Return the pan to a very low heat and cook for 3 minutes, continuing to fork through the grains.

4 Transfer the couscous to a bowl and stir through the remaining 2 tablespoons of olive oil and the juice of both lemons, seasoning well with sea salt and freshly ground black pepper.

5 Snap the bottom 2–3 cm off the base of the asparagus stalks and discard, then cook the asparagus in boiling water for 1 minute. Drain then refresh under cold water to prevent the asparagus from cooking further. Cut into 2 cm pieces on the diagonal and add to the couscous.

6 Add the gremolata chicken to the couscous and toss gently to combine. This salad will transport quite happily all made up.

CRUSHED POTATOES *with* FETA, LEMON, ROCKET *and* OLIVES

SERVES 4

This salad can either be eaten as a meal on its own or served as part of a selection of dishes.

800 g small salad (new) potatoes,
   larger ones halved
2½ tablespoons olive oil
100 g pancetta or prosciutto
2½ tablespoons lemon juice
handful flat-leaf parsley,
   roughly chopped
small handful mint, roughly torn
20 pitted kalamata olives, halved
100 g rocket leaves
180 g Persian feta or other
   soft feta, drained if in oil,
   and broken into small pieces

1 Put the potatoes into a large saucepan of salted water. Bring to the boil then reduce the heat and simmer for about 15 minutes or until the potatoes are tender when pierced with the tip of a sharp knife. Be careful not to overcook them.

2 Meanwhile, heat 1 teaspoon of the oil in a frying pan over medium heat. Add the pancetta and fry for 3–4 minutes, until crispy. Remove from the pan and set aside.

3 Drain the potatoes well and leave them to cool for 5–10 minutes. Transfer them to a clean tea towel and wrap them up. Using your palms, gently squash the potatoes to crack them open a little. Tip them into a large bowl.

4 While the potatoes are still warm, combine the remaining olive oil and lemon juice, and season well with sea salt and freshly ground black pepper. Pour this mixture over the potatoes and toss gently to combine. Set aside to cool.

5 Roughly chop the pancetta, then add it to the potatoes once they are cool, along with the parsley, mint, olives and rocket leaves, tossing gently to combine. Scatter with the feta and serve.

6 If transporting, take the rocket and feta separately and toss through just before serving.

ALL WRAPPED UP

NOTHING BEATS a well-thought-out sandwich – fresh bread filled with equally fresh ingredients – but sometimes it's hard to think outside what you normally have for lunch. For a picnic, a hike or an old-fashioned afternoon tea, the humble sandwich needs to be something a little more special.

As well as delicious, outside-the-square sandwiches, this chapter includes some Asian-inspired ideas where the filling is enclosed neatly inside a rice-paper wrapper. I've made bread suggestions for the sandwiches, but feel free to use your own favourite loaf or experiment with something new.

PRAWN *and* LIME MAYONNAISE ROLLS

MAKES 4 ROLLS

Sometimes the simple things in life are the best. Juicy prawns smothered in a tangy lime and herb mayonnaise make the perfect sandwich filling for a summer's day.

1 baguette, cut into 4,
    or 4 panini rolls
150 g good-quality egg mayonnaise
about 1 tablespoon lime juice
200 g peeled cooked prawns,
    deveined and roughly chopped
    (450 g unpeeled raw prawns)
small handful mint leaves,
    finely chopped
small handful coriander leaves,
    finely chopped
80 g rocket leaves

1 Slice the baguette or rolls almost all the way through along the top and open up. Spread both sides with some mayonnaise.

2 Stir most of the lime juice into the remaining mayonnaise, checking the taste and consistency before adding the rest of it; don't make it too runny. Stir in the prawns, mint and coriander. Season well with sea salt and freshly ground black pepper.

3 Divide the rocket between the bread then top with the prawn–mayonnaise mixture.

4 Wrap each roll in a piece of baking paper, twisting the ends to enclose (see styling tip). Chill until needed. Transport in an esky (cool box).

☞ STYLING TIP

Tie the twisted ends of the baking paper with some lovely string or ribbon.

TUNA *and* EGG PAN BAGNAT

MAKES 4–6 PORTIONS

Pan bagnat is a sandwich from the Nice region of France, and is sold in pretty much every market and bakery in the area, usually in a round roll. It's ideal to take on a hike or even a stroll to your local park for a picnic, because the flavours develop as you walk. It often contains green capsicum (pepper) and anchovies, so feel free to add these too if you like.

3 free-range eggs
80 ml (⅓ cup) olive oil
2 tablespoons red wine vinegar
1 teaspoon dijon mustard
1 long (40–50 cm) baguette
1 garlic clove, halved
1 baby cos lettuce, leaves separated
1 tomato, thinly sliced
185 g tinned tuna (in oil or spring
    water), drained and flaked
20 pitted kalamata olives, halved

1 Cook the eggs in boiling water for 7½ minutes. Plunge into cold water to stop them cooking. Cool, then peel. Carefully cut into wedges.

2 Whisk together the olive oil, vinegar and mustard until well combined. Season with sea salt and freshly ground black pepper.

3 Slice the baguette in half lengthways, leaving a hinge on one side, then open out flat. Remove a little of the dough from the bottom half to make a place for the filling to sit. Brush both sides of the bread with a little of the olive oil dressing, then rub the cut side of the garlic all over the bread.

4 Arrange the lettuce leaves across the bottom of the baguette, then top with the tomato, tuna, egg and olives. Drizzle with the remaining dressing then carefully close up, ensuring all the filling is kept inside the baguette.

5 Wrap the whole baguette in baking paper and then foil, and seal tightly. Store in the fridge until needed or heading off on your walk. If it's easier to transport in individual portions, cut and wrap before leaving home.

☞ STYLING TIP

Not only will your sandwiches look more stylish tied with rustic twine, but stacking coils of colourful string and twine also makes a simple but effective shelf display.

☞ **STYLING TIP**
If you collect interesting objects, try to incorporate them into your table settings.

A SELECTION of BEAUTIFUL SANDWICHES for AFTERNOON TEA

EACH FILLING MAKES 4 SANDWICHES OR 8 SMALL ROLLS

No afternoon tea in the garden, on the banks of a river or at the races is complete without a plate of delicate sandwiches. Cut off the crusts then slice each sandwich into fingers.

POACHED CHICKEN AND BASIL

250 g boneless, skinless chicken breast (or 200 g cooked chicken), preferably free range
120 g good-quality egg mayonnaise
1 tablespoon small capers, rinsed, drained and rinsed again, finely chopped
8 slices wholemeal or white bread, or 8 small soft rolls
softened butter, for spreading
16 large basil leaves
½ lemon

1 Halve the chicken breasts horizontally to make them thinner so they'll cook more quickly. Place in a saucepan and just cover with water. Bring to the boil, reduce the heat and gently simmer for 5 minutes. Remove from the heat and leave to cool and finish cooking in the poaching liquid.

2 Combine the mayonnaise and capers and season with sea salt and freshly ground black pepper. Finely shred the cooled chicken into the bowl. Spread each piece of bread with butter then top half the slices with the chicken mixture and add four basil leaves to each. Squeeze a little lemon juice over the filling, ensuring no lemon pips fall into it. Top with the remaining bread and press down gently. Slice off the crusts and cut into fingers or triangles.

EGG AND CRESS

3 free-range eggs
60 g crème fraîche or sour cream
2 tablespoons mint, finely chopped
softened butter, for spreading
8 slices wholemeal or white bread, or 8 small soft rolls
small box of cress or micro herbs

1 Cook the eggs for 7½ minutes in simmering water. Drain and plunge into cold water. Leave to cool, then peel. Put into a bowl and mash. Add the crème fraîche and mint and season with sea salt and freshly ground black pepper.

2 Butter the bread then divide the egg mixture between half of the slices. Top with some cress and the remaining bread and press down gently. Remove the crusts and cut into finger sandwiches.

FRESH SALMON, CUCUMBER AND DILL MAYONNAISE

1 tablespoon olive oil

160 g fresh salmon fillet,
   pin bones removed

80 g good-quality egg mayonnaise,
   plus 2 tablespoons extra

2 tablespoons fresh dill,
   finely chopped

1 tablespoon lemon juice

8 slices wholemeal or white bread,
   or 8 small soft rolls

½ Lebanese cucumber, thinly sliced

1 Brush the oil all over the salmon and cook on a preheated chargrill pan or under a hot grill for 4–5 minutes on each side, or until just cooked through (the exact time will depend on how thick the salmon is). Set aside to cool.

2 Combine the mayonnaise, dill and lemon juice and season with sea salt and freshly ground black pepper. Flake in the salmon and mix gently.

3 Spread each slice of bread with a little of the extra mayonnaise then place six slices of cucumber on four of the bread slices, just in from the edges. Top with a layer of the salmon mixture, then top with the remaining bread, pressing down gently. Slice off the crusts and cut into finger sandwiches.

☞ **STYLING TIP**

Dressing up your table can be as simple and low-cost as displaying a small spray of delicate flowers in a jar or bottle.

CHICKEN TORTILLAS *with* AVOCADO *and* CHIPOTLE CHILLI SALSA

MAKES 8 TORTILLAS

For speed you can use ready-cooked chicken (poached, roasted or grilled) when making this recipe. Chipotle chillies are widely used in Mexican cooking and add a smoky as well as spicy flavour to food.

2 tablespoons soy sauce

2 tablespoons mirin (available from the Asian section in most supermarkets)

2 tablespoons runny honey

400 g boneless, skinless chicken breast, preferably free range, cut into thin strips

8 flour or corn tortillas

125 g sour cream

2 ripe avocados, thinly sliced

CHIPOTLE CHILLI SALSA

3 tomatoes, quartered

2 spring onions, finely chopped

4 tablespoons coriander leaves, finely chopped

1–2 chipotle chillies in adobo sauce, finely chopped (available from good delis and grocers; see tip)

1 tablespoon lime juice

1 Combine the soy sauce, mirin and honey in a bowl and add plenty of freshly ground black pepper. Add the chicken and toss to coat. Leave to marinate in the fridge for about 30 minutes or up to 6 hours.

2 Meanwhile, make the salsa. Discard the seeds from the tomatoes then dice. Gently combine with the remaining salsa ingredients (adding two chillies if you like it spicy), season with sea salt and set aside.

3 Preheat a barbecue flat plate or chargrill pan and cook the chicken in batches, until cooked through and very slightly blackened.

4 Warm the tortillas according to the packet instructions, to soften. Spread each tortilla with a thin layer of sour cream. Leaving a 1–2 cm gap top and bottom, arrange a layer of avocado up the middle.

5 Top with the chicken and some chipotle chilli salsa. Fold in the bottom, rotate 90 degrees, fold over one side, then roll up. Wrap in baking paper and foil to keep the tortillas extra leak-proof, and transport to your event.

6 Remove the foil and serve in the paper.

TIP Pronounced chi-pot-*lay*, chipotle chillies are most frequently sold in tins. Once a tin is opened, you can freeze individual chillies in small freezer bags for later use.

CHINESE ROAST DUCK RICE-PAPER ROLLS

MAKES 12 ROLLS

Rather than wrapping Peking roast duck in pancakes that can dry out, here it's enclosed in rice-paper wrappers. Served with a hoisin dipping sauce, this is something a bit different to take on a picnic or day out.

1 Chinese roast duck, sliced
   (see tip)
12 Vietnamese rice-paper wrappers
12 large sprigs of coriander, halved
3 spring onions, thinly shredded
   into 8–10 cm lengths
1 large Lebanese cucumber,
   cut into 8–10 cm batons
12 large mint leaves

DIPPING SAUCE
2 tablespoons hoisin sauce
1 tablespoon soy sauce
1 teaspoon sesame oil
1 red chilli, seeded and finely
   chopped (optional)

1 Combine the dipping sauce ingredients in a bowl and set aside.

2 Prepare the duck. It's up to you if you use the skin as well as the meat; I prefer to use only the meat. Either way, discard the bones and shred the meat and skin, if using.

3 Using one wrapper at a time, dip the wrapper briefly into a large shallow bowl of warm water. Do not leave it in for too long or it may tear. Allow excess water to drip off.

4 Place the wrapper on a board and put a sprig of coriander crossways on the bottom third of the wrapper. Top with a few pieces of duck, some shredded onion, four cucumber batons and a mint leaf. Ensure the filling is compact and neat, then turn up the bottom of the wrapper to cover the filling. Holding the filling in place with your fingers, carefully turn in both sides on top of the bottom fold. Gently but firmly roll everything up so it is quite tight. Turn the roll over so the sprig of coriander is visible through the wrapper.

5 Repeat with the remaining wrappers, keeping the assembled ones under damp paper towel to prevent them drying out. Store in the fridge or esky (cool box) until needed.

6 Serve accompanied by the dipping sauce.

TIP You can buy ready-cooked Chinese roast ducks from Asian roast-duck restaurants and takeaway venues. Ask them to slice the duck for you.

ITALIAN DELI-STUFFED LOAF

SERVES 6

Instead of making six separate sandwiches, make one large filled loaf and then slice it to serve – every slice is packed full of flavoursome ingredients. To save time you could buy the chargrilled vegetables from a deli or supermarket, although, I usually prefer to make my own. You could also use an oblong loaf if you can't find a round one.

1 large red capsicum (pepper), halved and deseeded (or 100 g bought chargrilled capsicum, drained)
1 large zucchini (courgette), halved and thinly sliced lengthways (or about 100 g bought chargrilled zucchini, drained)
2 tablespoons olive oil
1 round loaf, about 22 cm in diameter
1–2 tablespoons pesto
40 g rocket leaves
110 g buffalo mozzarella, sliced
100 g salami or good-quality ham, thinly sliced
handful basil leaves
1 tablespoon extra-virgin olive oil (optional)

1 Preheat grill to high. Squash the capsicum halves flat, then grill until the skin is blackened all over. Transfer to a plastic bag, seal the bag and leave for 15 minutes. Peel off the skin. Cut the capsicum into 2 cm wide strips.

2 Meanwhile, heat a chargrill pan over medium heat. Brush the zucchini slices on each side with oil and chargrill until softened.

3 Slice off the top of the loaf about 3 cm from the top and reserve this to use as a lid. Hollow out the loaf, leaving about a 2 cm border all the way around. (You can use the scooped-out bread to make breadcrumbs.)

4 Brush the entire inside of the bread and the bottom of the lid with pesto, and season with sea salt and freshly ground black pepper. Place the rocket in the base then top with the chargrilled zucchini, making an even layer. Top with the mozzarella, then the salami and next the red capsicum. Scatter with the basil leaves, and drizzle the extra-virgin olive oil over the top, if you like. Cover with the lid.

5 Wrap the loaf in plastic wrap and put on a plate. Place a second plate on top and put a tin or two on top of the plate to weigh it down slightly. Leave for 1 hour or up to 4 hours in the fridge to allow the flavours to develop.

6 Wrap the loaf in a clean tea towel to transport it, and slice into thick wedges to serve.

SICHUAN BEEF RICE-PAPER ROLLS

MAKES 8 ROLLS

Sichuan (also known as szechwan) pepper gives food a slightly citrusy flavour; you'll find it in Asian stores and some supermarkets. Rice-paper rolls are fun to make. If taking these to someone's house, you could take all the components separately and get everyone to roll their own.

250 g beef eye fillet
1–2 tablespoons olive oil
2 teaspoons sichuan peppercorns
2 tablespoons kecap manis (see tip)
1 tablespoon lime juice
2 teaspoons sesame oil
8 rice-paper wrappers
8 small crunchy lettuce leaves
2 carrots, cut into very thin batons
2 Lebanese cucumbers,
   cut into batons
handful of coriander leaves
8 garlic chives, cut in half

TANGY DIPPING SAUCE
1 tablespoon fish sauce
1 tablespoon lime juice
1 teaspoon rice vinegar
1 teaspoon sesame oil
2 teaspoons sugar
1 small red chilli, deseeded
   and finely chopped

1 Heat a chargrill pan or barbecue over high heat. Brush the beef all over with olive oil then cook for 2–3 minutes on each side, or until cooked to your liking. If the beef is particularly thick, cook it for a minute on the edges as well. Set aside to cool. Once cool, slice very thinly against the grain.

2 Meanwhile, toast the sichuan peppercorns in a frying pan for 1–2 minutes until aromatic, shaking the pan regularly. Then crush the peppercorns in a spice grinder or mortar and pestle until quite fine.

3 Combine the kecap manis, lime juice, sesame oil and sichuan peppercorns. Add the beef slices and toss to coat. Set aside.

4 Whisk together the dipping sauce ingredients, ensuring the sugar dissolves.

5 Using one wrapper at a time, dip the wrapper briefly into a large shallow bowl of warm water. Do not leave it in for too long or it may tear. Allow excess water to drip off.

6 Place the wrapper on a board and put a lettuce leaf horizontally across the middle, one third up from the bottom closest to you. Top with some carrot, three cucumber batons and a few pieces of beef, then with several coriander leaves. Fold the end closest to you over the filling, then fold in the sides. Put two pieces of garlic chives along the seam with about 4 cm sticking out the top, then roll up quite tightly. Repeat with the remaining wrappers, keeping the made ones under damp paper towel to prevent them drying out. Store in the fridge or esky (cool box) until needed.

7 Divide the sauce between a couple of serving bowls and serve when ready.

☞ **TIP** Kecap manis is a thick, dark, sweetened soy sauce available from Asian stores. If you can't find it, simply stir 1 tablespoon of brown sugar into 2 tablespoons of soy sauce instead.

CORONATION CHICKEN BAGUETTES
with CRUNCHY APPLE 'SLAW

MAKES 4–6 BAGUETTES

Coronation chicken is a dish that's often joked about as being old-fashioned, but I doubt you'll get any complaints with this version, served in a crusty baguette with crunchy coleslaw. This recipe makes sufficient filling for a baguette that's about 60 cm long. You could also use a couple of ciabatta loaves.

35 g (⅓ cup) flaked almonds
80 g good-quality egg mayonnaise
2 tablespoons sour cream
2 teaspoons Indian curry paste
    or 1 teaspoon curry powder
2 teaspoons tomato paste
1 tablespoon lemon juice
3 tablespoons mango or apricot
    chutney
300–350 g cooked chicken
    (poached, roasted or grilled),
    preferably free range
1 long (about 60 cm) sourdough
    baguette

CRUNCHY APPLE 'SLAW
1 green apple, cored, halved and
    cut into thin matchsticks
1½ tablespoons lemon juice
150 g white cabbage, core removed,
    finely shredded
handful coriander leaves,
    roughly torn
1 tablespoon olive oil

1 Heat a frying pan over medium heat. Add the almonds and toast for a few minutes until golden, shaking the pan regularly. Set aside to cool.

2 Whisk together the mayonnaise, sour cream, curry paste, tomato paste, lemon juice and chutney, then season with sea salt and freshly ground black pepper. Shred the chicken into bite-sized pieces and gently stir into the mayonnaise dressing with the almonds.

3 To make the coleslaw, put the apple pieces into a bowl, add 2 teaspoons of the lemon juice and toss to coat. Add the shredded cabbage and coriander. Combine the remaining tablespoon of lemon juice with the oil and season with sea salt and freshly ground black pepper. Add to the apple mixture and toss gently to combine.

4 Cut the baguette into four or six pieces then slice open, leaving a hinge at the back. Divide the coleslaw between the baguette pieces, then top with the chicken mixture. Wrap in baking paper, twisting the ends to secure.

5 Store in the fridge until needed and transport in an esky (cool box).

Bigger BITES

WHEN ASKED TO BRING a dish to an event, we often revert to our old favourites. So next time, why not branch out and try something different? Treat everyone to salted roast potatoes with three dips – I can guarantee the potatoes will be gone in a flash. Kids and adults alike will love the crumbed chicken with sticky dipping sauce, and if you're looking for something a little more sophisticated, try the prosciutto-wrapped prawns with garlic aïoli.

SMOKY MEXICAN CHICKEN

SERVES 4–6

Chipotle chillies add a delicious spicy and smoky flavour to food. They're sold in tins in adobo sauce and are worth hunting down from delis, specialist food stores and many online shops.

2 tablespoons olive oil,
    plus extra for chargrilling
1 tablespoon brown sugar
2 tablespoons apple juice
1 chipotle chilli in adobo sauce,
    finely chopped
2 garlic cloves, crushed
1 teaspoon dried oregano
500–600 g boneless, skinless
    chicken thighs, preferably free
    range, halved
lime wedges to serve

1   Combine the olive oil, sugar, apple juice, chipotle chilli, garlic and oregano in a bowl and season with sea salt and freshly ground black pepper. Add the chicken and toss to coat. Leave to marinate in the fridge for at least 1 hour or up to 4 hours.

2   Remove the chicken from the marinade, allowing any excess marinade to drip off.

3   Brush a barbecue or chargrill pan with oil then heat to medium–high. Cook the chicken for 5–6 minutes on each side, or until cooked through. Cut into smaller pieces to serve, if you like. Can be eaten hot or cold. Serve accompanied by lime wedges.

4   If you're taking these to a place that has a barbecue, take them uncooked then cook on arrival.

☞ STYLING TIP

If eating outside, the wind can sometimes carry your napkins away! Solve this problem by tying some colourful string or twine around an interesting-shaped rock, and use this to hold the napkins in place.

BAKED RICOTTA *with* ROASTED VEGETABLES

SERVES 6–8

It's best to use 'dry' ricotta for this dish, as it will bake better. Look for it in Italian delis and cheese shops.

2 large red capsicums (peppers),
  quartered and deseeded
  (or 200 g bought chargrilled
  capsicum, drained)
2 large zucchini (courgettes), halved
  and thinly sliced lengthways
3 tablespoons olive oil
1 large garlic clove, crushed
1 kg ricotta, preferably the dry type

whole basil leaves to garnish
120 g rocket leaves to serve
crusty bread to serve

1 Preheat grill to high. Squash the capsicum pieces flat, then grill until the skin is blackened all over. Transfer to a plastic bag, seal the bag and leave for 15 minutes. Peel off the skin. Cut into 2 cm wide strips.

2 Meanwhile, heat a chargrill pan over medium heat. Brush the zucchini slices on each side with oil and chargrill until softened. Set aside.

3 Preheat fan-forced oven to 180°C (200°C conventional/ Gas 6). Combine the garlic with 2 tablespoons of oil and season with sea salt and freshly ground black pepper. Brush the insides of a loaf tin (approximately 8 x 22 cm or with a 1.3 litre capacity) with the garlic-oil.

4 Arrange the zucchini slices in the base of the loaf tin, laying them lengthways and slightly overlapping, then brush with the garlic-oil. Top with the capsicum strips, laying them crossways, and brush with the garlic-oil.

5 Spoon the ricotta into the tin, pressing it down quite firmly and smoothing the top. Brush with the garlic-oil and place on a baking sheet. Bake for about 25 minutes or until firm and browned around the edges.

6 Leave to cool in the tin for 10 minutes then turn out onto a serving plate, rearranging any vegetables as necessary. Garnish with basil. Slice using a sharp knife, and spoon any juices over the top. Can be served warm or cold, accompanied by rocket leaves and crusty bread.

7 If transporting, leave to cool in the tin then turn out on arrival.

PORK, APPLE *and* FENNEL SAUSAGE ROLLS

MAKES 9 LARGE OR 18 MEDIUM SAUSAGE ROLLS

Sausage rolls are pretty quick to make, and homemade ones are usually superior to even the best ones available in shops. I like to make quite large ones and this is what this recipe specifies, however, if you prefer more dainty ones, use six sheets of puff pastry, divide the filling into six and bake for 15–20 minutes.

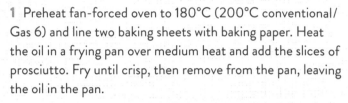

1 tablespoon olive oil

3 slices prosciutto

1 small onion, finely chopped

2 garlic cloves, crushed

500 g pork mince

2 tablespoons wholegrain mustard

1 apple, peeled and finely grated

2 teaspoons fennel seeds

60 g (1 cup) panko
   (Japanese breadcrumbs)

2 free-range eggs

3 sheets frozen puff pastry (about
   24 x 24 cm), thawed in fridge

1 Preheat fan-forced oven to 180°C (200°C conventional/ Gas 6) and line two baking sheets with baking paper. Heat the oil in a frying pan over medium heat and add the slices of prosciutto. Fry until crisp, then remove from the pan, leaving the oil in the pan.

2 Add the onion and garlic to the pan, reduce heat to low and cook gently until softened.

3 Cut the prosciutto into small pieces and put it into a bowl with the onion, garlic, pork mince, mustard, apple, fennel seeds, panko and one of the eggs, lightly beaten. Season well with sea salt and freshly ground black pepper and mix until thoroughly combined.

4 Lay one sheet of puff pastry on a board or clean work surface. Take one-third of the pork mixture and arrange along the bottom edge, about 2 cm in from the edge, ensuring it is of equal thickness all the way along. Brush the top edge of the pastry with the remaining beaten egg, then roll up the pastry from the bottom to enclose the filling. Seal quite firmly. Brush the pastry all over with egg and repeat with the remaining pastry and filling.

5 Using a sharp knife, cut the rolls into the desired size. I usually make either three large ones per roll (about 8 cm long) or six 4 cm ones. Place on the baking sheets, seams down, allowing room to expand slightly. Bake 4 cm ones for about 20 minutes and 8 cm ones for about 25 minutes, until the rolls are light golden and puffed. Cool on wire racks.

6 Transport in a lidded container with sheets of baking paper in-between the layers of sausage rolls.

SALTED ROAST POTATOES
with THREE DIPS

SERVES 4–6

Baby potatoes roasted in oil and salt have to be one of life's ultimate pleasures. Throw in a choice of dips and whoever you serve this to will be your friend for life. These dips are also brilliant with crudités.

2 tablespoons olive oil

1 kg small salad (new) potatoes,
    scrubbed, larger ones halved

1 tablespoon sea salt flakes

2 rosemary sprigs,
    broken into pieces

1 x quantity garlic aïoli (page 114)

ROASTED BEETROOT AND GARLIC DIP

1 large raw beetroot, unpeeled,
    trimmed top and bottom

1 small whole bulb of garlic

1 tablespoon olive oil

1 tablespoon sour cream

HERBED SOUR CREAM AND HORSERADISH DIP

150 g sour cream

2 tablespoons chives, snipped

3 teaspoons horseradish (from a jar)

1 Preheat fan-forced oven to 180°C (200°C conventional/ Gas 6). Wrap the beetroot and whole bulb of garlic in foil and place on a baking sheet. Roast the garlic for 50–60 minutes, or until it feels very soft, and the beetroot for 1½–2 hours, or until very tender when pierced with the tip of a knife.

2 Meanwhile, for the potatoes, put the oil in a large roasting tin and heat in the oven for 5 minutes. Add the potatoes, 2 teaspoons of sea salt and the rosemary, and toss to shake everything around. Roast for about 50 minutes or until tender.

3 Allow the beetroot to cool slightly, then, wearing rubber gloves to prevent staining, rub off the skin. Roughly chop and put into the bowl of a food processor with the oil. Snip off the tops of the garlic cloves and squeeze the purée from each clove into the food processor bowl. Season with sea salt and freshly ground black pepper and blend until smooth. Add the sour cream and blend briefly. Check the seasoning again. Transfer to an airtight container to transport.

4 To make the sour cream dip, soften the sour cream by beating it with a fork, then stir in the chives and horseradish and season with sea salt and freshly ground black pepper. Store in an airtight container.

5 Serve the potatoes hot, warm or cold sprinkled with the remaining 2 teaspoons of salt and accompanied by the dips.

SHREDDED PORK TOASTS

SERVES 6

This is my take on the traditional French dish rillettes, which has been around for centuries but still has a welcome place at today's table. Served on toast with onion jam and cornichons, it's a definite crowd-pleaser. Another advantage is that it can be made a few days in advance and stored in the fridge.

1 kg boneless, skinless pork belly,
   cut into 3–4 cm cubes
2 teaspoons table salt
2 large garlic cloves,
   slightly squashed
1 bay leaf
¼ teaspoon ground nutmeg
1 teaspoon juniper berries
1 large sprig of thyme

toast or crusty bread to serve
1 x quantity onion jam (page 50)
   to serve
cornichons (gherkins) to serve

1 Preheat fan-forced oven to 140°C (160°C conventional/ Gas 2–3). Put the pork into a casserole dish that fits the cubes quite snugly and sprinkle with the salt. Push the garlic cloves between the pork pieces, then add the bay leaf, nutmeg, juniper berries and thyme. Season well with freshly ground black pepper. Add 150 ml of water, cover with a lid and cook for about 3 hours, or until lots of fat has been released and the pork is very tender.

2 Remove the pork from the pan, reserving the juices and fat. Remove the bay leaf, juniper berries and thyme, but leave the garlic in.

3 Finely shred the pork using two forks, then add three-quarters of the pan juices and garlic and mash everything together. Check the seasoning, adding additional salt and pepper if required, as it should be well seasoned.

4 Pack into either six small glass jars or ramekins or two larger ones, smoothing the top. Pour the remaining cooking juices over the top. If the jars have lids, put them on; otherwise cover with plastic wrap. Refrigerate until needed; these will keep for up to three days in the fridge.

5 Serve accompanied by toast triangles or crusty bread, onion jam and cornichons.

☞ STYLING TIP

Soak off the labels from new and old jars and use the jars for serving food. A range of different shapes and sizes looks best.

☞ **STYLING TIP**
Coloured ribbon, textured twine and quirky fabrics add fun to your styling.

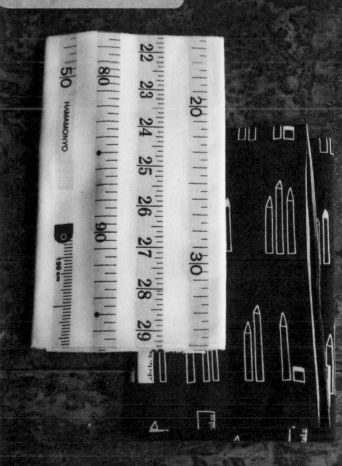

CRUMBED CHICKEN *with* STICKY DIPPING SAUCE

MAKES ABOUT 15 PIECES OF CHICKEN

The large, crispy panko (Japanese breadcrumbs) used in this recipe give the chicken a really crisp coating, while the dipping sauce is rich, sticky and totally delicious!

800 g boneless, skinless chicken breast, preferably free range
1–2 free-range eggs
90 g (1½ cups) panko (Japanese breadcrumbs)
2 tablespoons coriander, finely chopped
2–3 tablespoons olive oil

STICKY DIPPING SAUCE
1 tablespoon vegetable oil
2 garlic cloves, crushed
2 cm piece ginger, finely grated
100 ml hoisin sauce
1 tablespoon soy sauce
2 tablespoons sweet chilli sauce

1 Make the sauce first to allow it time to cool. Heat the oil in a small frying pan, then add the garlic and ginger and fry gently for about 2 minutes. Add the remaining ingredients, 2 tablespoons of water and a good grinding of freshly ground black pepper (no salt). Stir to combine, then bring to the boil. Remove from the heat and leave to cool. This sauce will keep for two to three days in the fridge.

2 Cut each piece of chicken into long strips (although they can be cut into smaller bite-sized pieces, if you prefer). Put one of the eggs into a shallow dish and lightly beat. Combine the panko and coriander in a bowl and season with sea salt and freshly ground black pepper, then tip half onto a large plate.

3 Preheat fan-forced oven to 180°C (200°C conventional/ Gas 6). Line a baking tray with baking paper and put it into the oven while the oven heats up. Dip each piece of chicken into the egg, allowing any excess to drip off. Then dip into the panko mixture, coating on all sides. Use the second egg and remaining panko as needed – keeping it in two batches stops the breadcrumbs from becoming soggy!

4 Heat the oil in a large frying pan over medium heat. Add the chicken pieces a few at a time and cook for 1–2 minutes on each side, until the breadcrumbs start to brown.

5 Transfer the chicken to the hot baking tray and bake for 8–10 minutes. Serve warm or cold with the dipping sauce.

6 If taking these somewhere that has an oven, you may like to take them raw but ready crumbed then cook on arrival. Or you could cook them at home then reheat them in the oven before serving.

PROSCIUTTO-WRAPPED PRAWNS
with GARLIC AÏOLI

MAKES 20 PRAWNS

Once cooked, these prawns are dipped into a homemade garlic aïoli. You could, of course, buy a jar of aïoli but your homemade version will taste far superior. If you're taking these to a place where there's a barbecue, prepare them before you leave then cook them on arrival. Otherwise, cook them beforehand and eat cold.

20 medium raw king prawns,
   peeled and deveined, tails left on
100 g prosciutto
olive oil, for brushing

GARLIC AÏOLI
3 garlic cloves, roughly chopped
1 teaspoon sea salt flakes
2 free-range egg yolks, at room
   temperature
250 ml (1 cup) lightly flavoured
   olive oil
3–4 teaspoons lemon juice

1 Soak 20 wooden skewers (preferably about 20 cm long) in water for 20 minutes.

2 To make the aïoli, put the garlic into a medium bowl with the salt. Using the back of a fork, mash the garlic and salt together until a paste forms.

3 Add the egg yolks and, using an electric hand mixer, mix until a thick paste forms. With the mixer in motion, start adding the olive oil, drop by drop; don't be tempted to add it faster, otherwise the aïoli may split. Once the aïoli becomes thick and creamy, you can add the oil in a steady stream. (This process should take 10–15 minutes, so don't rush it.) Add the lemon juice to taste and check the seasoning, adding extra salt if needed. Put into the fridge until required.

4 Thread each prawn onto a wooden skewer. Cut the prosciutto into long strips approximately 3 cm wide, then, starting just above the tail, wrap a strip around each prawn, leaving 1 cm of prawn visible at the top. Brush with olive oil.

5 Cook the prawns on a chargrill pan or on the flat plate of a barbecue for about 2 minutes on each side, or until the prawns are cooked through. Serve the prawns hot, warm or cold with the aïoli dipping sauce.

6 If transporting, the prosciutto-wrapped prawns can be taken uncooked and then cooked at your destination, or cook and chill them before you go. Transport in a lidded container in an esky (cool box).

MANCHEGO *and* OLIVE TORTILLA

SERVES 6–8

This substantial tortilla is made with sliced potatoes, creamy crème fraîche and
rich manchego cheese. It's easy to transport and then slice on arrival.

about 850 g potatoes, peeled
   and thinly sliced
10 free-range eggs, lightly beaten
150 g crème fraîche or sour cream
small handful flat-leaf parsley,
   roughly chopped
150 g manchego cheese, grated
50 g pitted green olives,
   roughly chopped

green salad to serve
1 x quantity onion jam (page 50)
   or shop-bought chutney to serve
   (optional)

1 Line the base and side of a 22 cm springform
(or loose-based) cake tin first with a layer of foil and
then a layer of baking paper. Preheat fan-forced oven
to 170°C (190°C conventional/Gas 5).

2 Cook the potatoes for 5 minutes in boiling, salted water
to soften. Drain well. Cool slightly then layer half into the
base of the tin.

3 Combine the eggs, crème fraîche and flat-leaf parsley
and season well with sea salt and freshly ground black pepper.
Pour about half the mixture over the potatoes then scatter
with half the cheese and all the olives. Scatter the remaining
cheese over the olives, top with the remaining potatoes,
then pour the remaining egg mixture over the top.

4 Bake for 40–45 minutes or until firm, set and golden.
Cool for 10 minutes in the tin, then very carefully open
the sides but leave the sides around the tortilla. Leave to
cool completely.

5 For easy transportation, carefully fit the sides around
the base again. Slice into wedges on arrival and serve with
a fresh green salad. Onion jam or chutney make a delicious
accompaniment.

TIP Leftover tortilla
is delicious for lunch the next
day; wrap it in baking paper to
prevent it falling apart while
transporting.

Artfully MOVEABLE

HOW TO TRANSPORT FOOD you've prepared to take somewhere needs consideration, from a simple packed lunch to a complete 'moveable feast'. Some countries have this perfectly sorted: think of the Japanese bento and the Indian tiffin. These traditions have been around for centuries and are still in use today – in both these countries you can see people carrying their lunch to work in these containers, or lunch delivery people with their bicycles or scooters piled high with bento and tiffin.

With the help of this chapter you can create your own Indian or Japanese feast to go, and there are also the makings of a delicious Spanish tapas spread.

INDIAN TIFFIN

Indian flavours are some of my favourites. The following recipes make up a feast featuring tandoori prawns, a classic potato salad and a refreshing tomato salad. I love the spice of chilli tempered by cool yoghurt. None of these recipes are particularly spicy though, so if you prefer spicy food, add the extra green chilli to the potato salad.

SPICED POTATO AND CHICKPEA SALAD WITH RAITA DRESSING

SERVES 6 AS PART OF A MEAL

2 large potatoes, peeled and halved
400 g tinned chickpeas, drained, rinsed and drained again
1 teaspoon chaat masala (see tip)
2 spring onions, finely chopped
1 tablespoon coriander leaves, finely chopped
1 tablespoon mint leaves, finely chopped
1 firm ripe tomato, deseeded and diced
1 green chilli, deseeded and finely chopped (optional)

RAITA DRESSING

½ teaspoon ground cumin
250 g Greek-style natural yoghurt
handful mint leaves, finely chopped
1 small garlic clove, crushed
1 small green chilli, deseeded and finely chopped
1 Lebanese cucumber, halved lengthways, deseeded and grated

1 Boil the potatoes until tender, then drain and set aside until cool enough to handle. Cut into small dice and put into a bowl with the chickpeas.

2 Sprinkle the chaat masala over the potatoes and chickpeas, and toss gently to combine. Add the spring onion, coriander, mint, tomato and chilli (if using), and stir gently to combine.

3 To make the raita dressing, heat a dry frying pan over medium heat. Add the cumin and toast for 1 minute, stirring regularly. Tip into a bowl and add the remaining ingredients and a big pinch of salt. Stir well.

4 Just before serving, spoon about three-quarters of the dressing over the potato and chickpea salad. Serve the remaining dressing on the side.

5 If transporting, take the salad and dressing in separate containers and combine just before serving.

☞ TIP
Chaat masala is an Indian spice mix containing ingredients such as mango powder and ground cumin. It's available from Indian supermarkets, but if you can't get it, use garam masala instead.

TOMATO AND ONION RELISH

SERVES 6 AS PART OF A MEAL

2 large or 3 medium firm,
    ripe tomatoes
½ red onion, diced
1–2 tablespoons lemon juice
small handful coriander leaves,
    roughly chopped
½ teaspoon garam masala

1 Cut the tomatoes into quarters and scoop out and discard the seeds. Dice the flesh and put it into a small bowl.

2 Add the remaining ingredients and a good pinch of salt, and set aside for about 30 minutes to allow the flavours to develop. Transport in an airtight container.

TANDOORI PRAWNS

SERVES 6 AS PART OF A MEAL

2 teaspoons ground cumin

100 g Greek-style natural yoghurt

1 tablespoon fresh ginger,
   finely grated

2 garlic cloves, crushed

2 tablespoons lemon juice

½ teaspoon garam masala

50 g unsalted butter

24 medium raw king prawns,
   peeled and deveined, tails left on

lemon wedges to serve

coriander sprigs to serve (optional)

1 Heat a dry frying pan over medium heat. Add the cumin and toast for 1–2 minutes, stirring regularly. Tip into a bowl and stir in the yoghurt, ginger, garlic, lemon juice and garam masala. Set aside for 10 minutes.

2 Melt the butter in a large frying pan over medium heat. Once it has melted and is bubbling, add the yoghurt mixture and cook, stirring for 2 minutes or until you can see the butter separate from the yoghurt and the sauce is thick.

3 Increase the heat to high, add the prawns and cook, stirring regularly for 3–4 minutes until the prawns are bright pink and cooked through. Remove from the heat and tip into a shallow dish. Set aside to cool in the sauce. Transfer to an airtight container for transporting.

4 Serve garnished with lemon wedges for squeezing over the prawns, and sprigs of coriander.

JAPANESE BENTO

Making sushi isn't as daunting as many people think, and generally your freshly made sushi will taste vastly superior to most that you buy. The simple edamame side salad is delicious with other Japanese flavours, but is also a great accompaniment to cooked meat or fish, and the teriyaki chicken salad is pretty quick to make once the chicken has been marinated.

EDAMAME SALAD WITH PICKLED GINGER

SERVES 6 AS PART OF A MEAL

450 g edamame beans, fresh or
   frozen (thawed), in pods (see tip)
2 tablespoons pickled ginger, finely
   chopped
large handful rocket leaves

DRESSING
1 tablespoon Japanese rice vinegar
1 tablespoon light olive oil
1 tablespoon mirin (available
   from the Asian section in most
   supermarkets)
2 teaspoons soy sauce
pinch of sugar

1 Cook the beans (in their pods) in boiling water for 2 minutes. Drain and refresh under cold water. Pop the beans from the pods into a bowl.

2 Combine the dressing ingredients in a separate bowl, stirring well to dissolve the sugar.

3 Combine the beans, pickled ginger and rocket leaves. Put into a lidded bowl or storage container and pour the dressing over the top.

4 If it will be more than 30 minutes before the salad is eaten, transport the rocket in a separate container and add just before serving, otherwise the dressing will make the leaves soggy.

☞ **TIP**   Edamame beans are Japanese soy beans. They're often found in the freezer section of supermarkets or in Asian supermarkets. You usually eat them by themselves with salt, but they're also delicious in salads.

TERIYAKI CHICKEN AND NOODLE SALAD

SERVES 6

3 tablespoons soy sauce (preferably
   Japanese shoyu, but not vital)
2 tablespoons mirin (available
   from the Asian section in most
   supermarkets)
2 tablespoons runny honey
2 teaspoons sesame oil
2 garlic cloves, crushed
5 cm piece ginger, grated
600 g boneless, skinless chicken
   breast, preferably free range
oil for chargrilling
300 g soba noodles
100 g snow peas (mangetout),
   shredded
4 spring onions, thinly sliced
   on the diagonal

DRESSING

2 tablespoons Japanese rice vinegar
1 tablespoon light olive oil
1 tablespoon mirin
2 teaspoons soy sauce
1 teaspoon sugar
½ teaspoon sesame oil

1   To make the teriyaki marinade, combine the soy sauce, mirin, honey, sesame oil, garlic and ginger in a small bowl. Add a good grinding of freshly ground black pepper, but don't add salt as the soy sauce is already salty.

2   Cut each chicken breast into two pieces and any particularly thick pieces in half horizontally to make thinner pieces, then make a couple of slashes across each piece. Add the chicken breasts to the marinade and turn to coat well. Leave to marinate in the fridge for at least 1 hour or up to 12 hours.

3   Remove the chicken from the marinade, allowing any excess marinade to drip off. Heat an oiled chargrill pan, barbecue flat plate or grill to medium and cook the chicken, turning regularly, for 10–12 minutes, or until just cooked through. Set aside to cool (the chicken will cook a little further while cooling, so don't overcook it).

4   While the chicken is cooling, cook the noodles according to the packet instructions. Then drain and rinse briefly under cold running water. Drain well then transfer to a large bowl.

5   Combine all the dressing ingredients, stirring to dissolve the sugar. Pour the dressing over the noodles (see step 7) and toss well to coat the noodles.

6   Once the chicken is cool, shred into bite-sized pieces. Add to the noodles with the snow peas and half the spring onions. Toss to combine then scatter with the remaining onions.

7   If transporting, reserve half the dressing. Transport the salad and extra dressing in lidded containers. Dress the salad with the remaining dressing just before serving.

SALMON AVOCADO SUSHI WITH SESAME-WASABI MAYONNAISE

**MAKES 6 LONG ROLLS OR
48 BITE-SIZED PIECES**

2 teaspoons sesame seeds
2–3 tablespoons Japanese
    mayonnaise or good-quality
    egg mayonnaise
1 teaspoon wasabi
400 g (2 cups) Japanese sushi rice
3 tablespoons Japanese rice vinegar
6 sheets nori (dried seaweed)
300 g sashimi-grade salmon, cut
    into 1 cm wide lengths (see tip),
    or 2 x 185 g tinned tuna in
    spring water
1 ripe avocado, thinly sliced
soy sauce to serve

☞ TIP

It's vital that you use
sashimi-grade salmon as
you are eating raw fish.
Many fish shops and fish
markets sell this. If you
can't get it, make tuna
sushi, using tinned fish,
instead. Nori and wasabi
can be found in the Asian
section of supermarkets.

1 Heat a dry frying pan over medium–high heat and toast the sesame seeds for 1–2 minutes until golden. Transfer to a small bowl to cool. Once cool, add 2 tablespoons of the mayonnaise and the wasabi and stir to combine, making sure the wasabi is thoroughly mixed in. (If making tuna sushi, mix the tuna into the mayonnaise as well and add an extra 1 tablespoon of mayonnaise.)

2 Cook the rice as per the packet instructions or in a rice cooker. Transfer to a shallow dish and add the rice vinegar. Stir gently so as not to crush the grains of rice and fan to cool, using a piece of cardboard or a newspaper.

3 Place a sushi mat onto a clean work surface with the slats running horizontally. Place a sheet of nori, shiny side down, on the mat, with the lines running horizontally. Put a small bowl of water next to you and lightly wet your fingers. Take a small amount of cooled rice and gently push it onto the nori. Lightly wet your fingers again and repeat with more rice until you have covered almost all the nori with a thin layer of rice (with no holes), leaving about a 3 cm wide border along the top edge. The trick here is to not add too much rice at a time and to make sure your fingers are slightly wet or your hands will get covered in rice!

4 Spread a little sesame-wasabi mayonnaise about 3 cm up from the bottom edge (if making tuna sushi, form a sausage shape on the rice with one-sixth of the tuna mayonnaise mixture instead). Top with one salmon strip (or sufficient to cover the width) and one line of sliced avocado. Pick up the bottom edge of the mat and, holding the filling in place using your fingertips, roll up the sushi using the mat to help, but ensuring the mat doesn't end up inside the roll. Once rolled, use the mat to help form a tight, neat roll.

5 Unroll the mat and place the sushi, seam side down, on a board or plate and repeat with the remaining seaweed sheets, rice and filling to make five more rolls.

6 Using a very sharp knife, trim each end of the sushi rolls then cut each of them into eight pieces. Arrange on a platter and serve with soy sauce.

7 If transporting, you may want to leave the rolls whole and then slice on arrival (don't forget the knife). If transporting sliced, gently cover the cut edges with plastic wrap.

☛ **STYLING TIP**
Old glass jars and bottles can
be used decoratively around the
house, to transport food and to
display beautiful objects.

SPANISH TAPAS

Sharing food with friends and family is one of life's great pleasures, and the Spanish certainly know a thing or two about this. Prepare a couple of salads, some hearty empanadas and some delicious marinated olives – and perhaps throw in a bottle of rioja – then head out and enjoy your feast, savouring the food over the course of an afternoon.

BROAD BEANS WITH RED CAPSICUM AND SPANISH HAM

**SERVES 6–8 AS PART
OF A TAPAS MEAL**

1 red capsicum (pepper)
1 tablespoon olive oil
1 onion, finely chopped
3 garlic cloves, crushed
200 g jamon serrano or prosciutto,
    roughly chopped
500 g broad beans, fresh or frozen
    (thawed), podded then slipped
    out of their skins
125 ml (½ cup) dry white wine
200 ml good-quality chicken stock
small handful flat-leaf parsley,
    roughly torn

1 Preheat grill to high. Put the capsicum under the hot grill until the skin is blackened all over, turning as it blackens. Transfer the capsicum to a plastic bag, seal the bag and leave for 15 minutes. Peel off the skin and remove the seeds and membrane, reserving any juices. Cut into short strips and set aside.

2 Meanwhile, heat the oil in a large frying pan and add the onion and garlic. Cook over a gentle heat for 3 minutes until softened and starting to brown. Add the jamon and cook for 3–4 minutes. Add the beans and wine, increase the heat and cook until the wine has reduced by about half. Add the stock, cover and simmer for about 5 minutes.

3 Remove the lid and simmer for a further 5 minutes or until the liquid has almost all evaporated. Transfer to a serving dish and set aside to cool. Once cool, season with sea salt and freshly ground black pepper, stir in the capsicum and its juices, and scatter with the parsley. Transport in an airtight container.

☞ STYLING TIP
Homemaker and craft stores sell an array of luggage-label-type accessories. Add instant colour with some pretty twine.

EMPANADAS

MAKES 14 EMPANADAS

1 tablespoon olive oil
40 g butter
1 small onion, finely chopped
3 spring onions, chopped
150 g beef mince
½ teaspoon ground cumin
½ teaspoon ground cinnamon
½ teaspoon chilli flakes
pinch of nutmeg
60 g manchego or tasty cheese, finely grated
2 hard-boiled free-range eggs, chopped
14 stuffed green olives, halved

PASTRY
450 g (3 cups) plain (all-purpose) flour
1 teaspoon table salt
100 g chilled butter, cubed
1 free-range egg

1 Put the oil into a large frying pan and heat over medium heat. Add 20 g of the butter and, just as it melts, add the onion and fry for about 3 minutes until softened. Add the spring onions and cook for 2 minutes. Stir in the beef, increase the heat and cook until just browned. Stir in the cumin, cinnamon, chilli flakes and nutmeg, season with sea salt and freshly ground black pepper and cook for 1 minute. Transfer to a bowl and leave to cool in the fridge for 30 minutes.

2 Meanwhile, make the pastry. Put the flour into a food processor with the salt and butter. Process until the mixture resembles fine breadcrumbs. Add the egg and 100 ml of cold water and pulse until the mixture starts to come together. Turn onto a floured work surface and knead briefly to form a smooth dough. Shape into a ball then flatten into a disc. Wrap in plastic wrap and chill for 20–30 minutes.

3 Preheat fan-forced oven to 180°C (200°C conventional/ Gas 6). Line two baking trays with baking paper. Halve the dough and roll out thinly on a floured work surface. Using a 15 cm cutter (or small plate) cut out seven circles, re-rolling the dough as necessary. Repeat with the second piece of pastry.

4 Gently stir the cheese into the beef mixture. Place tablespoons of the mixture into the centre of each pastry disc. Top with a little chopped egg and two olive halves. Brush the edges of the pastry with water, then fold the pastry in half to enclose the filling, gently sealing the edges. Crimp the edges by gently twisting them between your thumb and forefinger. Sit the empanadas up flat, so the crimp is at the top, and place them on the prepared baking trays. Melt the remaining 20 g of butter and brush the empanadas with it. Bake for 25 minutes until golden. Serve warm or cold.

CHORIZO AND CHICKPEA SALAD

**SERVES 6–8 AS PART
OF A TAPAS MEAL**

2 tablespoons olive oil
250 g chorizo, thinly sliced
1 onion, halved and thinly sliced
2 garlic cloves, crushed
2 thyme sprigs
2 x 400 g tinned chickpeas,
    drained, rinsed and drained again
½ lemon

1 Heat the oil in a frying pan and add the chorizo. Fry for 5 minutes, turning to brown both sides. Remove from the pan, leaving the oil in the pan. Add the onion and garlic to the frying pan and cook for about 5 minutes. Return the chorizo to the pan with the thyme.

2 Add the chickpeas and 125 ml (½ cup) of water. Season with sea salt and freshly ground black pepper. Cover with a lid and cook gently for 5 minutes, shaking the pan regularly, until the chickpeas are warmed through.

3 Transfer to a serving dish and leave to cool. Squeeze the lemon over the salad just before serving.

4 If transporting, use an airtight container – and don't forget the lemon.

MARINATED OLIVES

**SERVES 6–8 AS PART
OF A TAPAS MEAL**

250 g mixed green and black olives
2 garlic cloves, thinly sliced
1 red chilli, thinly sliced
2–3 thyme sprigs
2–3 oregano sprigs
125 ml olive oil

1 Put the olives in a bowl. Add the garlic, chilli, thyme and oregano. Drizzle with the olive oil and gently combine.

2 Put in the fridge and leave to marinate for at least 2 hours, but preferably a day or two.

3 If transporting, you may want to remove some of the oil, which you can keep and use for salad dressing or shallow frying.

Something SWEET

LET'S FACE IT: although afternoon tea is the obvious time to serve one of the delectable treats in this chapter, a cake, slice or meringue is welcome at pretty much any time of the day. Serve your 'something sweet' on a pretty plate accompanied by the perfect cup of tea, coffee or a glass of champagne.

There's something here for everyone. Kids will love the lemon and passionfruit melting moments, chocolate lovers will devour the orange and almond choc-truffle squares, and summer fruit lovers can choose between the poached stone fruit and the nectarine puff pastry tartlets.

POACHED STONE FRUIT *with* HONEYED MASCARPONE *and* ALMONDS

SERVES 6

Poached fruit is the perfect finish to a meal, as it's not too heavy. In summer poach peaches or nectarines, while in autumn and winter, plums work equally well. If you have a choice, don't buy any variety of clingstone fruit, as it will be very hard to halve before cooking.

juice of 1 orange
juice of 1 lime
35 g (¼ cup) caster sugar
3 star-anise
6 cardamom pods, squashed to split
1 vanilla bean, split
6 peaches or nectarines or
   10 plums, halved and stoned
35 g (⅓ cup) flaked almonds
250 g mascarpone
3 tablespoons milk
2 tablespoons runny honey

1 Put 250 ml (1 cup) of water into a wide, deep frying pan or large saucepan with the orange juice, lime juice, sugar, star-anise and cardamom pods. Scrape the seeds from the vanilla bean into the pan, then pop the pod in too. Bring to the boil, stirring to dissolve the sugar.

2 Reduce the heat to a very gentle simmer and add the fruit halves, cut side up. Cover the surface with a disc of baking paper and then a lid, and simmer for about 5 minutes until the fruit is tender. Leave to cool in the syrup.

3 Heat a frying pan over medium heat. Add the almonds and toast for 2–3 minutes until light golden, shaking the pan regularly.

4 Combine the mascarpone and milk to soften the mascarpone, then stir in the honey. Serve the fruit with a little syrup, the honeyed mascarpone and some almonds scattered over the top.

5 If transporting, place the fruit and syrup in a leak-proof container. Take the honeyed mascarpone and almonds in separate containers.

LEMON *and* PASSIONFRUIT MELTING MOMENTS

MAKES 15 MELTING MOMENTS

Here's one for kids and adults alike. If you don't like passionfruit seeds, sieve them before adding to the butter and lemon rind.

250 g butter, at room temperature
50 g icing sugar, sifted
1 teaspoon vanilla extract
250 g plain (all-purpose) flour,
    plus a little extra for dusting
60 g corn flour

FILLING
2 passionfruit, halved
60 g butter, at room temperature
finely grated rind of 1 lemon
110 g icing sugar, sifted

1 Preheat fan-forced oven to 150°C (170°C conventional/ Gas 3) and line two baking sheets with baking paper. Using a stand mixer or electric hand mixer, whisk the butter, icing sugar and vanilla extract together for 4–5 minutes, until pale and creamy. Sift in the plain flour and corn flour and, with the mixer on a very low speed, gradually whisk into the butter mixture. Stop mixing when it is just combined and you have a soft dough.

2 Lightly flour your hands then take teaspoon-sized portions of the mixture and roll them into balls. Place onto the prepared trays about 5 cm apart. Dip a fork into some flour, then gently flatten each ball to about 1 cm high. Bake for about 18–20 minutes until the biscuits are very light golden. Leave to cool on the baking sheets.

3 Meanwhile, make the filling. Scoop the passionfruit pulp into a bowl with the butter and lemon rind. Using an electric mixer, whisk until combined. Add half the icing sugar and whisk again until combined, then whisk in the remaining icing sugar until the sugar has dissolved. Refrigerate until it has firmed up.

4 Spread half the biscuits with a layer of the filling then sandwich together with a second biscuit. Store in an airtight container until required; they should last 3–4 days.

PISTACHIO MERINGUES
with CARAMEL FILLING

MAKES ABOUT 22 MERINGUES

I love meringues; they're a favourite from Sunday afternoon tea when I was a child. Instead of the traditional cream filling, I've filled these ones with caramel. Look for caramel in a can (often called Top 'n' Fill) in the baking section of supermarkets, or you can easily make your own caramel using condensed milk.

4 free-range egg whites
220 g caster sugar
2 teaspoons corn flour
1 teaspoon white vinegar
40 g pistachios, roughly chopped

CARAMEL FILLING
380 g caramel in a can
    or 395 g tinned condensed milk

1 If you don't have caramel in a can, make the caramel filling first. Remove the label from the condensed milk tin and make two small holes in the top. Put the tin into a saucepan and fill the saucepan with water up to 2 cm below the top of the tin (be careful not to let any water get into the holes). Bring to a simmer, uncovered, and keep simmering for 4 hours. You'll need to keep an eye on the water level and top it up with boiling water as necessary. Never let the pan run dry, otherwise your tin may explode! Carefully remove the tin from the pan and leave to cool completely.

2 Meanwhile, preheat fan-forced oven to 140°C (160°C conventional/Gas 2–3) and line three baking sheets with baking paper. Put the egg whites into a clean, grease-free bowl and, using a stand mixer or electric hand mixer, beat them until soft peaks form. Gradually add the sugar, 1 tablespoon at a time, whisking well after each addition. Whisk until the mixture is smooth and glossy. Fold in the corn flour, vinegar and three-quarters of the pistachios.

3 Put the mixture into a piping bag with no tube (or a zip-lock bag with the corner snipped off). Pipe small rounds (about 5 cm in diameter) onto the prepared trays, allowing a little room for expansion, and sprinkle with the remaining pistachios. Reduce the oven temperature to 130°C (150°C conventional/Gas 2) and bake for 40 minutes. Turn the oven off and leave the meringues inside to cool completely.

4 Scoop the caramel out of the tin, whisking it briefly to soften it. Use it to sandwich the meringues together.

5 These meringues are fine to transport filled. Don't squash them into a tin, but equally ensure they don't have too much room to move about, otherwise they may break.

☞ **STYLING TIP**

Craft shops sell chalkboards, which you can jazz up with some ribbon and write a fun message on or the name of the dish at afternoon tea.

PISTACHIO MERINGUES

FLOURLESS CHOCOLATE CAKE

SERVES 6–8

Using ground almonds instead of flour, this cake is light, moist and even a little bit chewy. It's pretty simple to make and has a hint of orange. You can serve it on its own or make it a bit more elegant by serving with strawberries and thickened cream.

vegetable oil for greasing
200 g 75% cocoa solids dark
  chocolate, broken into pieces
200 g unsalted butter, cubed
250 g caster sugar
5 free-range eggs, separated
230 g ground almonds
finely grated rind of 1 orange
cocoa powder or icing sugar to dust

strawberries to serve (optional)
thickened cream to serve (optional)

1 Grease the base and side of a 23 cm springform (or loose-based) cake tin and line the base with baking paper. Put the chocolate into a heatproof bowl and sit the bowl over a pan of barely simmering water, ensuring the base of the bowl isn't touching the water. Heat gently, stirring occasionally until the chocolate has melted.

2 Add the butter to the chocolate a quarter at a time, stirring occasionally. Add the next batch each time the butter has melted. Stir well to combine. Set aside for 10 minutes to cool slightly. Preheat fan-forced oven to 170°C (190°C conventional/Gas 5).

3 Put the sugar and egg yolks into a large bowl and, using a stand mixer or electric hand mixer, whisk for 4–5 minutes until pale and creamy. Wash the beaters. Put the egg whites in a clean grease-free bowl and whisk until stiff peaks form.

4 Once the chocolate mixture has cooled slightly, stir it into the egg-yolk mixture. Then fold in the ground almonds and orange rind. Stir 2 tablespoons of the egg whites into the mixture to loosen, then gently fold in the remaining egg whites.

5 Pour into the prepared tin and bake for about 35–40 minutes or until the cake is starting to pull away from the sides. Leave it in the tin for 10 minutes, then remove from the tin and leave to cool completely on a wire rack.

6 Dust with cocoa powder or icing sugar to serve, and cut into wedges accompanied by strawberries and cream, if you like. Otherwise serve it on its own.

MOCHA *and* HAZELNUT ECLAIRS

MAKES 12–14 ECLAIRS

'Yum' is pretty much the only way to describe these eclairs. With a coffee filling and chocolate and nuts on top, they're certain to disappear fast.

100 g (⅔ cup) plain (all-purpose) flour
60 g butter, cubed
½ teaspoon salt
3 free-range eggs
20 g hazelnuts
100 g good-quality dark chocolate, broken into pieces
15 g butter

COFFEE FILLING
150 ml thickened or whipping cream
1 tablespoon icing sugar, sifted
150 g crème fraîche
2 tablespoons cold espresso coffee (or 2 tablespoons instant coffee dissolved in 1 tablespoon of boiling water, chilled)

1 Line two large baking trays with baking paper. Sift the flour onto one of the pieces of paper. Put the butter into a saucepan with the salt and 160 ml (⅔ cup) of water. Bring to the boil, stirring occasionally, ensuring the butter melts before the water boils.

2 Remove from the heat and, using the baking paper like a funnel, quickly pour the flour into the boiling mixture (then use the paper to line the baking tray again). Return to the heat and beat vigorously with a wooden spoon until the mixture leaves the sides of the pan and forms a ball. Transfer to a bowl and leave to cool for about 15 minutes or until lukewarm.

3 Preheat fan-forced oven to 180°C (200°C conventional/ Gas 6). Using a stand mixer or electric hand mixer, beat in the eggs one at a time (reserving about 2 teaspoons of one of the eggs), until the mixture is thick and glossy.

4 Fit a piping bag with a 2 cm plain nozzle and fill the bag with the mixture. Pipe 12–14 lines about 2 cm wide and 10 cm long (6 cm apart) onto the trays. Brush with the remaining egg.

5 Bake for 10 minutes (see tip), then reduce the temperature to 150°C (170°C conventional/Gas 3) and bake for a further 15 minutes, until the eclairs are golden brown and puffed. Remove from the oven and carefully cut each eclair along one side (scissors work well for this), around the top and down the other side (be careful as hot steam will escape) to separate into two pieces. Turn the oven off and return the eclairs to the oven for a further 5 minutes to dry out. Set aside to cool. ☞

6 Meanwhile, toast the hazelnuts in a frying pan over medium heat for 2–3 minutes until golden. Cool then roughly chop. Melt the chocolate and butter together in a microwave, or in a heatproof bowl set over a pan of barely simmering water. Stir until glossy.

7 To make the coffee filling, use an electric mixer to whisk the cream and icing sugar together until stiff peaks form. Fold in the crème fraîche and coffee, then whisk again to stiffen the mixture. Spoon into a piping bag fitted with a 1 cm plain or fluted nozzle. Top the eclair bottoms with the filling.

8 Spread the eclair tops with the melted chocolate and scatter with the nuts, then put the tops on the bottoms. Chill for 20 minutes or until the chocolate has set.

9 Transport in a single layer. If making more than an hour in advance, add the coffee filling at your destination, but the tops can be chocolate-coated before leaving home. Eat within 2–3 hours of filling.

☛ **TIP**   If your oven bakes at a lower temperature on the lower shelf than the top, bake one tray of eclairs at a time – they're okay to sit for a while unbaked.

☛ **STYLING TIP**
Add a vintage feel to your afternoon tea with an old-fashioned jar filled with marshmallows.

NECTARINE PUFF PASTRY TARTLETS
with FRANGIPANE FILLING

MAKES 8 TARTLETS

Nectarines are one of my favourite summer fruits; I love them especially for their amazing colours. I also love the purple tinge of the pistachios used in this recipe, but it's fine if you don't want to add them. The nectarines sit on a delicious frangipane (almond) filling.

2 sheets frozen puff pastry (about 24 x 24 cm), thawed in fridge

4 firm, ripe nectarines, stoned and sliced into eight pieces

2 tablespoons apricot jam, melted

30 g (¼ cup) pistachios, roughly chopped

1 small free-range egg, lightly beaten

icing sugar to dust (optional)

FRANGIPANE FILLING

50 g unsalted butter

50 g caster sugar

1 small free-range egg, lightly beaten

50 g ground almonds

1 tablespoon plain (all-purpose) flour

½ teaspoon almond extract

1 To make the frangipane filling, put the butter and sugar into a food processor and blend for about 30 seconds until creamed together. Add the egg, ground almonds, flour and almond extract and blend well, scraping down the sides of the bowl once. Transfer to a small bowl. Preheat fan-forced oven to 180°C (200°C conventional/Gas 6).

2 Cut each sheet of puff pastry into quarters. Using a sharp knife, cut a shallow border 1 cm in from the edge of each piece, ensuring you don't cut all the way through the pastry. This will enable the pastry border to puff up around the filling when it bakes. Place onto two baking trays lined with baking paper. Spread the frangipane filling inside the border then chill for 15 minutes.

3 Top the frangipane with the nectarine slices, brush with the jam and scatter with pistachios. Brush the pastry borders with the egg. Bake for 20 minutes, or until the tartlets are puffed and golden.

4 Serve warm or cold, dusted with icing sugar, if you like. If transporting, either bake the tartlets beforehand and serve them cold on arrival, or, if you're going somewhere with an oven, assemble and chill them before leaving home then bake them at your destination.

RASPBERRY CAKE

SERVES 8

If you're not a particularly confident baker, this is the cake for you – it looks great but is pretty simple to make. Fresh or frozen raspberries can be used, so it can be made all year round (I actually prefer to use frozen as they're often juicier). Serve it as a simple slice of cake or accompanied by cream as more of a dessert.

120 g salted butter, softened,
   plus extra for greasing
185 g (1 cup lightly packed)
   brown sugar
3 free-range eggs, lightly beaten
60 ml (¼ cup) milk
1 orange, grated rind and
   2 tablespoons juice
225 g (1½ cups) plain (all-purpose)
   flour
1 teaspoon baking powder
200 g raspberries, fresh or
   frozen (thawed)
icing sugar to dust
thickened cream to serve (optional)

1 Preheat fan-forced oven to 180°C (200°C conventional/ Gas 6). Butter and lightly flour the side of a 23 cm springform (or loose-based) cake tin.

2 Using a stand mixer or electric hand mixer, beat the butter and sugar for 4–5 minutes, until creamy. Gradually add the eggs, beating well after each addition, then whisk in the milk. The mixture may look like it has curdled but it should be fine when the flour is added.

3 Stir in the orange rind and juice, then sift in the flour and baking powder and fold through. Gently fold through half the raspberries. Spoon the mixture into the prepared tin, smoothing the top. Scatter the remaining raspberries over the top, pressing them gently into the batter.

4 Bake for 30 minutes until the cake has risen and is golden. Leave in the tin for 10 minutes, then remove from the tin and cool on a wire rack. Dust with icing sugar and serve in slices, accompanied by thickened cream, if liked. This cake is best eaten the day it is made.

5 If transporting, return the cake to the tin to keep it safe.

☞ STYLING TIP
Old cutlery doesn't have to match and adds charm to your table setting.

DIVINE LEMON *and* LIME TARTLETS

MAKES 8 TARTLETS

What makes these divine? A tart lemon and lime filling encased in a rich, buttery pastry, that's what. If you don't have time to make the pastry, you'll need about 500 g of shop-bought, sweet shortcrust pastry.

PASTRY

225 g (1½ cups) plain (all-purpose)
  flour
80 g (½ cup) icing sugar
finely grated zest of 1 lemon
100 g chilled butter, cubed
2 free-range egg yolks
1 tablespoon chilled water

FILLING

60 ml (¼ cup) lemon juice
  (about 2 lemons)
30 ml lime juice (1 or 2 limes)
125 ml (½ cup) thickened cream
80 g caster sugar
2 free-range eggs, lightly beaten

250 g mascarpone cheese
2 tablespoons milk
1 tablespoon icing sugar,
  plus extra to dust

1 Sift the flour onto a sheet of baking paper on a work surface, then sift the icing sugar on top. Using the paper like a funnel, tip the flour and sugar into the bowl of a food processor. Add the lemon zest and butter and blend until the mixture resembles fine breadcrumbs. Add the egg yolks and briefly blend until the mixture just starts coming together. Add the water and blend briefly again.

2 Tip the mixture into a bowl and bring together. Form it into a ball then squash into a disc and wrap in plastic wrap. Chill for about 1 hour.

3 Preheat fan-forced oven to 170°C (190°C conventional/ Gas 5). Divide the pastry into eight equal portions. Roll out each portion between two sheets of baking paper (to make moving it easier) to a circle about 13 cm in diameter. Use the rolled-out pastry to line eight tartlet tins. Chill for 20 minutes. Line each tin with baking paper then fill with baking beans or raw rice. Place on a baking sheet and bake for 10 minutes. Remove the paper and beans and bake for a further 10 minutes.

4 While the pastry is baking, make the filling. Put the lemon and lime juice, cream, sugar and eggs in a large jug and whisk to combine. Pour into the pastry cases and bake for 12–15 minutes until just set (the filling will wobble a bit). Cool to room temperature then chill in the fridge until needed.

5 Combine the mascarpone, milk and icing sugar. Dust the tartlets with icing sugar and serve accompanied by the mascarpone mixture.

6 If transporting, leave the tartlets in their tins to protect the pastry shells.

INDIVIDUAL HONEYCOMB CHEESECAKE SLICES

MAKES 18 SMALL OR 12 MEDIUM SLICES

This is a rich and creamy cheesecake that will have everyone coming back for more. And, even better, it can be prepared in less than 20 minutes.

vegetable oil for greasing
200 g wholemeal (digestive)
   biscuits
110 g butter, melted
500 g full-fat cream cheese
125 g (½ cup) crème fraîche
   or sour cream
1 teaspoon vanilla extract
75 g (⅓ cup) caster sugar
3 teaspoons powdered gelatine
3 x 50 g bars chocolate-coated
   honeycomb (Crunchie),
   finely chopped

1 Grease a 16 x 26 cm slice tin and line with baking paper. Put the biscuits into a food processor and blend to fine crumbs. Tip into a bowl and add the melted butter, stirring until well combined. Transfer to the prepared tin, pressing into the tin and smoothing the top with the back of a spoon. Refrigerate while making the filling.

2 Put the cream cheese, crème fraîche, vanilla extract and sugar into a bowl and, using a stand mixer or electric hand mixer, beat together until smooth.

3 Put 2 tablespoons of hot water into a small bowl and sprinkle with the gelatine. Stir to dissolve. Beat into the cream-cheese mixture, then stir in three-quarters of the chocolate-coated honeycomb until thoroughly mixed through.

4 Pour over the biscuit base and smooth the top with a blunt knife. Scatter the remaining honeycomb over the top, then refrigerate for several hours (or overnight) until set, bearing in mind this isn't a particularly firm filling. Lift out of the tin using the paper to help. Trim any messy edges then slice into 12 or 18 pieces.

5 If transporting, leave the cheesecake in the tin and slice it on arrival.

HAZELNUT *and* RASPBERRY ROULADE

SERVES 6–8

Many roulades are made from meringue, but that type can be quite hard to roll. This one is softer and more cake-like, so is easier to roll and transport. It may crack slightly but that's fine – just dust the crack with extra icing sugar! You can also fill it with chopped strawberries or blackberries.

vegetable oil for greasing
6 free-range eggs, separated
180 g caster sugar, plus extra
   for sprinkling
1 teaspoon vanilla extract
50 g self-raising flour
70 g ground hazelnuts
icing sugar to dust

FILLING
1 tablespoon icing sugar
150 g thickened or whipping cream
100 g crème fraîche
½ teaspoon vanilla extract
125 g raspberries, fresh or
   frozen (thawed)

1 Preheat fan-forced oven to 180°C (200°C conventional/ Gas 6). Grease a Swiss roll tin (approximate dimensions 30 x 24 x 2.5 cm) and line with baking paper.

2 Put the egg yolks and sugar into a large bowl and, using a stand mixer or electric hand mixer, whisk for 5–6 minutes until pale and thick. Stir in the vanilla extract. Sift in the flour then fold in gently with the ground hazelnuts.

3 Using clean beaters, whisk the egg whites in a separate bowl until soft peaks form. Gently fold into the hazelnut mixture with a large metal spoon until just combined. Pour into the prepared tin. Bake for 15–20 minutes until golden and springy.

4 While the roulade is cooking, place a tea towel on a work surface then top it with a large sheet of baking paper and sprinkle with caster sugar. When cooked, carefully turn the roulade out onto the sugared paper and carefully peel off the paper that was in the baking tin. Trim the edges of the roulade to neaten, if necessary. Using the sugared paper to help you, roll up the roulade from the long side, enclosing the paper as you go. Leave to cool completely.

5 To make the filling, sift the icing sugar into the cream, then whisk until soft peaks form. Fold in the crème fraîche and vanilla extract. Gently stir through the raspberries.

6 Unroll the roulade and spread with the raspberry-cream filling. Re-roll the roulade. Place on a serving plate and dust with icing sugar. If transporting, dust with icing sugar just before serving.

ORANGE *and* ALMOND CHOC-TRUFFLE SQUARES

MAKES ABOUT 28 SQUARES

These are extremely rich and absolutely divine so you only need a small piece – a little goes a long way.

vegetable oil for greasing
100 g slivered almonds
150 ml pouring cream
200 g good-quality dark chocolate, broken into pieces
200 g good-quality orange dark chocolate, broken into pieces
50 g butter, cubed
cocoa powder to dust

☞ STYLING TIP

Wrap a few squares of this truffle in baking paper and tie with twine. It's the perfect way to say thank you, happy birthday or merry Christmas.

1 Grease a 16 cm square tin (or similar dimensions) and line with baking paper. Toast the almonds in a dry frying pan over medium heat for 2–3 minutes until lightly golden. Set aside to cool.

2 Put the cream into a small saucepan and bring just to boiling. While the cream is heating, put both chocolates into a heatproof bowl over a saucepan of barely simmering water, ensuring the bowl doesn't touch the water.

3 Pour the cream over the chocolate, add the butter and stir gently every now and then to melt the chocolate and combine well. Do not overheat the chocolate or it will seize and be ruined. Once the chocolate is completely melted, remove from the heat, stir until lovely and glossy and then stir in the almonds.

4 Pour into the prepared tin then refrigerate until firm (about 2–3 hours).

5 Carefully remove from the tin and dust with cocoa powder. Using a sharp knife, cut the choc-truffle into small pieces about 4 x 2 cm, cleaning the knife every so often. If taking it on a picnic, you might find it easiest to return it to the tin to transport. Keep it out of the sun!

STRAWBERRY *and* PASSIONFRUIT MERINGUE CAKE

SERVES 8

Meringue always looks impressive, and this slightly chewy version filled with strawberries and a hint of passionfruit is no exception.

6 free-range egg whites, at room temperature
250 g caster sugar
1½ teaspoons white vinegar
1 teaspoon vanilla extract
35 g (⅓ cup) ground hazelnuts
icing sugar to dust

FILLING
300 ml thickened cream
2 passionfruit, halved
250 g strawberries, roughly chopped

1 Preheat fan-forced oven to 140°C (160°C conventional/ Gas 2–3). Line two baking sheets with baking paper, then draw a 22 cm circle on each. Place paper drawing side down.

2 Using a stand mixer or electric hand mixer, whisk the egg whites in a clean grease-free bowl until stiff peaks form. Gradually add the sugar, whisking well after each addition to dissolve the sugar. Continue beating until the mixture is thick and glossy. Briefly whisk in the vinegar and vanilla extract. Gently fold in the ground hazelnuts.

3 Divide the mixture between the two circles and smooth the surface. Bake for 35–40 minutes. Then turn the oven off and leave the meringues to cool completely in the oven.

4 Remove the baking paper and place one meringue disc on a serving plate. To make the filling, whisk the cream until stiff peaks form, then scoop out the passionfruit pulp and stir into the cream. Spread over the meringue disc and scatter the strawberries over the top. Top with the second meringue and dust with icing sugar.

5 If you don't feel confident transporting the cake assembled, take the meringues and filling separately and put everything together on arrival. Remember to take the icing sugar for dusting.

DRINKS

SOMETIMES IT'S FUN to concoct a cocktail –
or a mocktail for those who have to drive – and
making a drink from scratch shows you've put
in that extra bit of effort. If entertaining adults,
serve these drinks in a beautiful jug with
pretty glasses, while kids will love cute
bottles with fun straws.

None of these drinks are hard to make. My
absolute favourite is the mojito beer, a long
refreshing drink perfect on a hot summer's day,
and the passionfruit fizz is always a hit with kids.

LEMONADE *with* LEMON SLICE ICE CUBES

MAKES 600–800 ML

If taking this drink on a picnic you won't be able to take the lemon slice ice cubes (unless you're going very close by), so make the lemonade in advance and chill well in the fridge. If serving in the garden or somewhere local, the ice cubes add a fun touch.

½ lemon
220 g (1 cup) sugar
300 ml fresh lemon juice
(from 6–7 lemons; see tip)

1 Make the lemon slice ice cubes a day in advance. Cut the lemon half into five thin slices, then cut each slice into quarters. Place one quarter into each hole of one or two ice-cube trays and fill with water. Freeze.

2 To make the sugar syrup, put 125 ml (½ cup) of water into a saucepan and bring to the boil. Add the sugar and stir to dissolve. Once completely dissolved, remove from the heat and allow to cool completely. The liquid will thicken slightly on cooling.

3 Put the lemon juice into a jug and stir in the sugar syrup. Add about 500–700 ml of water and stir. The amount of water you add will depend on how sweet you like the drink, so taste as you add the water. Serve chilled with plenty of lemon slice ice cubes.

TIP Roll the lemons on a work surface before juicing them, to increase the amount of juice you'll get. Rolling them breaks down the cell walls inside, releasing more juice.

PASSIONFRUIT FIZZ

MAKES 800 ML–1 LITRE

This is a very refreshing non-alcoholic drink for a sunny summer's afternoon, brilliant for anyone having to drive home from a picnic or day out. Kids love it too.

12 passionfruit, halved
4 tablespoons sugar
4 tablespoons lemon juice
500–600 ml sparkling water
ice cubes
1 lime, cut into thin wedges

1 Scrape out the seeds and pulp from the passionfruit and place in a blender with the sugar and lemon juice. Blend until smooth, then strain through a sieve.

2 Store in a lidded container until needed and for transportation.

3 To serve, divide the passionfruit mixture between four glasses, then top up with the sparkling water and add ice cubes and a wedge of lime. Alternatively, put everything into a jug and allow guests to help themselves. For kids, serve in cute bottles with fun straws.

SPARKLING RASPBERRY LEMONADE COCKTAIL OR MOCKTAIL

MAKES 1.8 LITRES

This works both as an alcoholic and non-alcoholic drink. Make up the base with the sparkling water then serve as is, or add a shot of vodka or gin for an extra hit.

500 g frozen raspberries, thawed
170 g caster sugar
250 ml (1 cup) lemon juice
   (about 3–4 lemons)
1.2 litres chilled sparkling water
vodka or gin (optional)
mint leaves to garnish
lemon slices to garnish

1 Put the raspberries into a food processor with the sugar, and blend to combine. Pour into a sieve placed over a bowl. Push the raspberries through the sieve using the back of a spoon (to remove the seeds).

2 Stir in the lemon juice. Transfer to a large jug and stir in the sparkling water.

3 If making an alcoholic drink, add 20 ml vodka or gin per person and serve garnished with mint leaves and lemon slices.

ORANGE *and* CARDAMOM ICED TEA

MAKES 1.3–1.5 LITRES

This very refreshing drink with a subtle tea taste is a delight to imbibe on a warm sunny day. Make double the amount in summer and keep a bottle chilled in the fridge ready to cool you down at a moment's notice.

6 cardamom pods
3 Earl Grey tea bags (or
   1½ tablespoons Earl Grey tea
   leaves in an infuser)
strips of orange peel from 1 orange
375 ml (1½ cups) fresh orange juice
   (about 3 juicy oranges)
2 tablespoons sugar, plus extra
   to taste
½ orange to garnish

1 Squash the cardamom pods until they split. Put the split pods into a saucepan with the tea, orange peel, orange juice and sugar. Add 1 litre (4 cups) of water and bring slowly to the boil, stirring occasionally and squashing the tea bags (if using) gently every now and then.

2 Set aside to cool, tasting as it cools, and once the tea flavour is strong enough, remove the tea bags or infuser. Once cool strain into a jug, adding extra sugar if a sweeter tea is preferred.

3 Cut the orange half into thin slices, then halve each slice and use to garnish the glasses. Serve chilled and drink within one to two days.

☞ **STYLING TIP**

Look for old bottles in second-hand shops or wash and rinse small sparkling-water or fruit-drink bottles.

MOJITO BEER

MAKES ABOUT 1.6 LITRES

*Stay with me here – I know you're thinking this sounds dreadful, but believe me,
it is amazing! It's the perfect drink for a hot summer's day or evening.*

220 g (1 cup) caster sugar
160 ml white rum
3 limes, cut into thin wedges
40 mint leaves, plus 8 sprigs
ice cubes
1 litre lager beer

1 Put 125 ml (½ cup) of water into a saucepan and bring to the boil. Add the sugar and stir to dissolve. Remove from the heat and allow to cool completely. The liquid will thicken slightly on cooling.

2 Add the rum to the sugar syrup and stir to combine.

3 Divide three-quarters of the lime wedges and the mint leaves between eight tall glasses. Muddle the lime and mint leaves to release the lime juice and mint oils. Add ice cubes to each drink then pour the rum-sugar syrup over the top. Slowly top up each glass with the beer.

4 Pop in a sprig of mint and a couple of lime wedges and serve.

☞ **STYLING TIP**
Play a little with your drinks
and serve them with fun
cocktail stirrers, umbrellas
or swizzle sticks.

INDEX

ABOUT THE AUTHOR

WITH A LONG AND SUCCESSFUL CAREER as a food writer and stylist,
Katy Holder has always been passionate about cooking. Katy grew up in
London, but has lived in Sydney for many years. There's no better city
than Sydney for eating outside and this inspired Katy's mission to create
a cookbook of delicious recipes that are easily transportable. She has
been the food director of *Family Circle* magazine, ghost-written several
cookbooks and written for most leading Australian food magazines and
publishers. She is also the author of *Hungry Campers Cookbook*. Katy
currently writes the food pages for Australia's *marie claire* magazine.

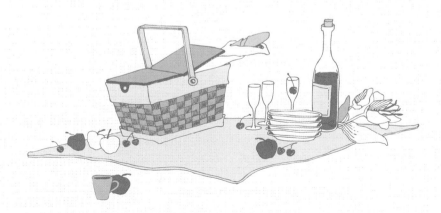

AUTHOR ACKNOWLEDGEMENTS

THE BIGGEST THANK YOU has to go to my amazing photography team, Tash and Grace. I cannot thank you enough for the long hours and hard work you put into creating this beautiful cookbook with me. Tash, you had constantly moving sunlight, pesky winds and two naughty cats (yes, that's you Bruce and Sheila) to contend with, but the book is proof that you took it all in your stride. Grace, your cooking skills and calm nature are legendary. Thanks also to Maria Madill for joining us on the shoot; I love that you just walk in, pick up a knife and start chopping.

Thanks to my family, Alex, Max and Jack, for tasting every recipe, often more than once or twice. Young Jack, you are fast becoming a food critic – I love your honesty!

Thank you to Melissa Kayser and Alison Proietto at Hardie Grant Explore for your guidance and for being so excited about the project. Thank you also to Debra Billson for her beautiful design, and to my editor Michelle Bennett for questioning the smallest detail.

PUBLISHER'S ACKNOWLEDGEMENTS

The publisher would like to acknowledge the following individuals and organisations:

Editorial manager
Melissa Kayser

Project manager
Alison Proietto

Editor
Michelle Bennett

Design and layout
Debra Billson

Photography
Natasha Milne

Home economist
Grace Campbell

Pre-press
Megan Ellis, Splitting Image

Illustrations appearing throughout the book and some backgrounds: Abimages/shutterstock.com; Kitigan/shutterstock.com; MyClipArtStore.com/shutterstock. com; IxMaster/shutterstock.com; lenaer/shutterstock.com; alicedaniel/ shutterstock.com; Irina Matskevich/ shutterstock.com; © Can Stock Photo Inc./freaksmg; © Can Stock Photo Inc./luceluceluce

With thanks to Mud Australia, Scout House and Spotlight for supplying props for use at the photo shoot.

Explore Australia Publishing Pty Ltd
Ground Floor, Building 1,
658 Church Street,
Richmond, VIC 3121 Australia

Explore Australia Publishing Pty Ltd is a division of Hardie Grant Publishing Pty Ltd

hardie grant publishing

Published by Explore Australia Publishing Pty Ltd, 2014

Form and design © Explore Australia Publishing Pty Ltd, 2014
Concept and text © Katy Holder, 2014

A Cataloguing-in-Publication entry is available from the catalogue of the National Library of Australia at www.nla.gov.au

ISBN-13 9781741174618

10 9 8 7 6 5 4 3 2 1

Printed and bound in China by 1010 Printing International Ltd

Disclaimer: This book uses metric cup measurements, i.e. 250 ml for 1 cup; in the US a cup is 8 fl oz, just smaller, and American cooks should be generous in their cup measurements; in the UK a cup is 10 fl oz and British cooks should be scant with their cup measurements.

Publisher's note: Every effort has been made to ensure that the information in this book is accurate at the time of going to press. The publisher welcomes information and suggestions for correction or improvement.
Email: info@exploreaustralia.net.au

www.exploreaustralia.net.au
Follow us on Twitter: @ExploreAus
Find us on Facebook:
www.facebook.com/exploreaustralia